BEST OF CHINA
YOUR #1 ITINERARY PLANNER FOR WHAT TO SEE, DO, AND EAT

Wanderlust Pocket Guides

Best of China

Planning a trip or looking for travel inspiration?
Check out our other Wanderlust Pocket Travel Guides on Amazon:

BEST OF BEIJING: YOUR #1 ITINERARY PLANNER FOR WHAT TO SEE, DO, AND EAT

BEST OF SHANGHAI: YOUR #1 ITINERARY PLANNER FOR WHAT TO SEE, DO, AND EAT

BEST OF HONG KONG: YOUR #1 ITINERARY PLANNER FOR WHAT TO SEE, DO, AND EAT

BEST OF JAPAN: YOUR #1 ITINERARY PLANNER FOR WHAT TO SEE, DO, AND EAT

BEST OF TOKYO: YOUR #1 ITINERARY PLANNER FOR WHAT TO SEE, DO, AND EAT

BEST OF KYOTO: YOUR #1 ITINERARY PLANNER FOR WHAT TO SEE, DO, AND EAT

BEST OF ITALY: YOUR #1 ITINERARY PLANNER FOR WHAT TO SEE, DO, AND EAT

BEST OF FLORENCE AND TUSCANY: YOUR #1 ITINERARY PLANNER FOR WHAT TO SEE, DO, AND EAT

BEST OF VENICE: YOUR #1 ITINERARY PLANNER FOR WHAT TO SEE, DO, AND EAT

BEST OF ROME: YOUR #1 ITINERARY PLANNER FOR WHAT TO SEE, DO, AND EAT

Our Free Gift to You

As purchasers of this paperback copy, we are offering you an **Amazon Matchbook download** of our colored **kindle version of this book for FREE.** Go to our book's page on Amazon and select the kindle version to download.

You **do not have to own a kindle** to read the kindle version of this book. Simply download the kindle reading app on your computer, tablet, or smartphone.

Great Wall of China, near Beijing

TABLE OF CONTENTS

HOW TO USE THIS GUIDE

Yangshuo, near Guilin

If planning an ordinary trip is already overwhelming enough, planning a trip to China may be more than any one person to handle – each region, province, or even city in this enormous country boasts of its unique character, history, culture, and people, with sights, experiences, and food that one cannot find even in the next city over. With so much on offer, it can be difficult to figure out what to include in your trip.

Luckily, this Wanderlust Pocket Guide is everything you need to plan an essential trip to China. You have a few ways to use the information here. You can choose to follow one of our itineraries, one of which takes you to Beijing and Shanghai, with a day trip to beautiful Hangzhou, while the other takes you additionally to the beautiful Guilin, with some of China's most stunning vistas, and the ancient capital, Xi'an, with the famous Terracotta Warriors.

Alternatively, we divide the cities and attractions we cover into "Ancient China", "Natural Wonders", "Modern China", and "Off-the-Beaten-Path". You can customize your own itinerary based on your interests. History lovers might decide to skip Shanghai in lieu of Suzhou, while those who love nature might decide to concentrate on Guilin.

In addition, we have a list of top experiences in China that any first-time visitor should make sure to seek out to make the most of the trip. In short, there are many ways to use the information in this guide, all written for you to customize your trip according to your interest. This is China after all, where you can find anything your imagination can conjure up, and much more besides!

INTRODUCTION

China is big, both literally and otherwise. Its 23 provinces, 5 autonomous regions, 4 municipalities, and 2 special administrative regions, cover over 9.6 million square kilometers, spanning 62 degrees of longitude and 49 degrees of latitude, with the world's highest mountains, biggest deserts, largest cities, and 14,500 kilometers of coastline. It also has the world's biggest population of 1.37 billion people of 56 ethnic groups, the ancestors of whom have been living in what is present day China for as long as 1.7 million years.

As well known today for its turbulent modern history as its ancient and proud culture, this once mysterious country has lately reemerged onto the world stage, and in recent years, embarked on a rapid evolution that has made it one of the most important players in world economics and politics. This dichotomy – being simultaneously old and new – is reflected in China's landscape. From the ultramodern skylines of Shanghai and Hong Kong, to the imposing imperial palace in Beijing; from the bustling shopping district on Nanjing Road, to the tranquil canals in Suzhou; from the trendy 798 Art Zone, to the Great Wall that has been guarding the country for millennia; some Chinese live in soaring high-rises, while others live in traditional courtyards. These two radically different faces of China are equally fascinating, and both are as true as the other.

Suzhou

Outside its major cities and urban tourist destinations, China offers some of the most beautiful vistas anywhere in the world, and as varied as its culture. There are peaceful lakes in the desolate highlands in Tibet, and vast and impassive deserts in Inner Mongolia; tropical islands that trick you into thinking you are in the Caribbean Islands, and rugged, unwelcoming mountains that once deterred invaders; picturesque karst pinnacles in Yangshuo, to dramatic river gorges in central China.

With so much to see and experience, China has become one of the most exotic and popular travel destinations around the world. While the relatively young People's Republic of China is still rough around the edges in some places, the country has increasingly opened its doors to welcome foreign travelers in recent years. More western style hotels are being built everyday, high-speed rail connects many important cities, and more and more people are learning English. Quite possibly, there has never been a better time to visit China, and with 120 million inbound tourists last year, you are in good company!

CHINA'S TOP EXPERIENCES

1. Climbing the Endless Great Wall of China

There is no more recognized symbol of China than the Great Wall. This truly monumental structure is a worthy representation of the enormity of the entire country. Visiting the Great Wall is one of the most "China" experiences there is. There are many points of interests along the wall. Some of the most well known spots are just outside Beijing, making them an ideal daytrip destination.

2. Stroll Along the Bund in Shanghai, Where the Old Meets the New

On one bank of the Huangpu River stand the magnificent and varied Art Deco buildings left during Shanghai's Colonial Era from the early 1900's, while on the other, ultramodern skyscrapers from the last few decades of China's rapid economic development soar into the clouds. At night, both old and new glitter with neon lights. A walk along this stretch of Shanghai's famous riverside, known as the Bund, is definitely a stunning experience that even those from the most metropolitan cities will be impressed, and unable to forget.

3. Gaze in the Lifelike Faces of the Terracotta Warriors

The scale of this famous group of ancient warrior statues is hard to imagine until you see it in person. There are thousands of them on display, along with terracotta horses, chariots and weapons, and many more still buried underground to protect them from damage. These are not cheaply mass-produced statues, but a real ancient Chinese army with different ranks of officers and different functions. Each statue is intricately carved with vivid details. It is rumored that no two faces are alike!

4. Visit the Forbidden City in Beijing

The Forbidden City is also known as the Palace Museum, but the former name is certainly more accurate: the residence of Ming and Qing Dynasty emperors and the center of the imperial Chinese government is no single palace, but actually an entire sprawling city within the city of Beijing. You can easily get lost here, where building follows after ornate building, alternating with garden after vivacious garden, all with tons of history in between.

5. Take a Boat Down the Li River with Views of the Karst Scenery

In a country full of natural beauty, Guilin's scenery is a serious contender for the top rank in China, or, as the famous sign says, in the world. As you travel to the nearby town of Yangshuo, emerald karst mountains flank the Li River on both sides of the similarly emerald water.

6. View the Super-Modern Hong Kong Skyline from Top of Victoria Peak

Brighter even than its counterpart in Shanghai or New York, the skyline in Hong Kong looks as if it has already arrived in the future. On top of Victoria Peak, you have a clear view of Victoria Harbor, the ultra-modern buildings, and the incredible music and light show each night.

7. **Marvel at the Potala Palace Against the Rugged Highland Vista of Tibet**
This red and white palace, the center of Tibetan Buddhism, is an imposing feature atop the Tibetan Highlands, which is nicknamed the "Rooftop of the World," watching over the land and people of Tibet. In the background are the vast and awe-inspiring mountains, and the clear blue sky that would have been a luxury nearly anywhere else in China. Whether you are a Buddhist pilgrim or not, this is a view that takes your breath away.

8. **Hold a Baby Panda in Your Arms in Chengdu**
Chengdu is the capital city of Sichuan Province, where the once abundant bamboo forests have been breeding these cute monochrome bears for eons. In recent years, pandas have become the world's most famous endangered species, but the reserve near Chengdu has helped to replenish the panda population, and has sent pandas to zoos across the world. You can see more pandas here than anywhere else in the world, and even hold a cub in your arms if you wish!

9. **Visit the West Lake in Hangzhou for its Poetic Scenery**
West Lake has inspired much art and poetry through its long popularity in China. Manmade elegance fuses perfectly with poetic landscape at each of the famous "scenes" in the area, each as splendid as a masterpiece, with a story and history as rich as Hangzhou itself.

10. Enjoy the Delicious, Exotic, Sometimes Weird Food
Depending on who you ask, China has the best, or the strangest eating habits. It would be a missed opportunity if you ate only McDonald's or sweet and sour pork (good luck finding it) while in China. Keeping food sanitation in mind, we suggest you try everything. There is precious little that the Chinese have not managed to make into a decadent dish.

BEST OF CHINA ITINERARIES

China at a Glance – 6 Days
Best of Beijing and Shanghai

Day 1 – 3: Beijing

Spend the first day in East City District. Start the morning by
snapping some photos in front of Tian'anmen Square, before
heading into the massive Forbidden City and admire the living
quarters of China's emperors. From there, take a walk to the
Temple of Heaven and the Drum and Bell Towers. Afterward,
look through the interesting boutique shops along Nan Luo Gu

Xiang for unique souvenirs. Have some Peking duck for dinner. If you are up for more, go for a drink lakeside in Hou Hai.

Head to Summer Palace on your second morning and admire the harmony between nature and architecture. Leave the Qing Dynasty for modern China after that, and head to Chaoyang District. You can look at the massive parks that were converted from the 2008 Beijing Olympic structures, visit a few galleries in 798 Art Zone, and shop for antiques in Pan Jia Yuan. End the day in San Li Tun Bar Street.

Reserve your third day in Beijing for the Great Wall. Most go to Ba Da Ling, but for a less crowded location, visit Mu Tian Yu.

For more details on visiting Beijing, find our Comprehensive **Best of Beijing** City Guide.

Day 4 – 5: Shanghai

Start with modern Shanghai in Pu Dong District. Pick one of the soaring towers for a panoramic view of the city. Walk through the area, before heading to the Yu Garden. The area has plenty of eating and shopping options along the streets, including the famous soup buns, known as "xiao long bao" in Chinese. Hop over to Xin Tian Di District after dinner and experience the nightlife – plenty of bars and live music.

On Day Two, head to People's Square. Spend a few hours looking through the valuable artifacts in Shanghai Museum. Walk along Nanjing Road and experience the bustling city atmosphere. End the day by taking in the nighttime view from the Bund.

For more details on visiting Shanghai, find our Comprehensive **Best of Shanghai** City Guide.

Day 6: Day Trip to Hangzhou

Board the speed train to Hangzhou in the morning and head to West Lake right away. Take a West Lake cruise for the most famous sights around here, before visiting Ling Yin Temple. After a lunch of West Lake cuisine, head to Six Harmonies Pagoda. Take the train back to Shanghai at the end of the day.

China in a Nutshell – 10 Days
Beijing - Xi'an - Shanghai - Hangzhou - Guilin

Day 1 – 3: Beijing

Follow the three-day itinerary in Beijing above.
For more details on visiting Beijing, find our Comprehensive **Best of Beijing** City Guide.

Days 4 – 5: Xi'an

Spend the morning with the Terracotta Warriors, the world's eighth wonder. In the afternoon, visit the Great Mosque, with its unique mixture of Islamic and Chinese influences. Explore the surrounding Muslim Quarter after for some delicious street food and fun souvenirs.

Walk around the ancient city walls on your second morning in Xi'an, or hire a bike. From there, visit the Big Wild Goose Pagoda. For more history, spend the rest of the day at the Shaanxi History Museum.

Day 6 – 7: Shanghai

Follow the three-day itinerary in Shanghai above.
For more details on visiting Shanghai, find our Comprehensive **Best of Shanghai** City Guide.

Days 8: Day Trip to Hangzhou

Follow the day trip itinerary to Hangzhou above.

Days 9: Guilin

Explore the most famous sights in Guilin, including Elephant Trunk Hill and Reed Flute Cave. Be sure to take a photo in front of "Guilin's Scenery Ranks First in the World." Take an evening Li River Cruise from Guilin to Yangshuo.

Day 10: Yangshuo

Explore the picturesque area all around Yangshuo. You can hike or bike through the fresh rural landscape. Later in the day, explore the many expats-run bars and restaurants and chat with someone from a different part of the world.

Have more time? Consider adding Hong Kong, Tibet and Chengdu to your itinerary. For more information on Hong Kong, find our Comprehensive **Best of Hong Kong** City Guide.

PLAN YOUR CHINA TRIP BASED ON YOUR INTERESTS

Best of Ancient China
Beijing
Xi'an

Best of China's Natural Wonders
Guilin
Chengdu

Best of Modern China
Shanghai
Hong Kong

Off the Beaten Path
Lhasa in Tibet
Hangzhou
Suzhou

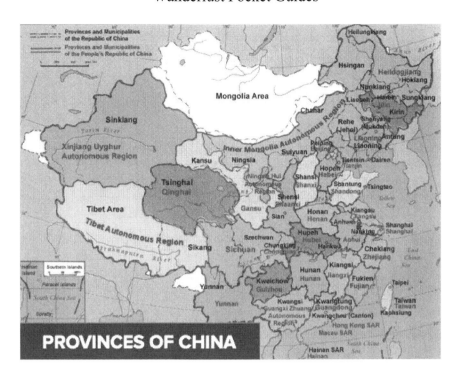

NORTH CHINA

Beijing

A trip to China is not complete without a visit to the most recent capital city of this ancient country. The name "Beijing" means "northern capital", a role it played many times in China's long history, until it became the official capital of the Ming and Qing Dynasties, and the seat of the emperors until the formation of a republic in 1911 that spelled the demise of the Qing Dynasty.

Today, Beijing is the second largest city after Shanghai, with 21.5 million people in the entire metropolitan area. It is the political, educational, and cultural center of the country as well, and home to many of the most important and popular historical sights that a visitor will want to see.

Beijing natives are fiercely proud of their historical and cultural heritage, and to be inhabitants of the country's capital city. There is an attitude known as "Great Beijing-ism" that describes their pride. They are often more interested in politics and are keen to discuss current events with you. Compared to people from Shanghai, Beijingers are considered humorous, friendly, and straightforward.

Beijing Municipality is a large area that is as sizeable as some provinces, and contains a densely populated metropolis and a greater area that incorporates suburban, sem-rural, and mountainous terrain.

Central Beijing where most visitors stay consists of five districts – East City, West City, Chaoyang, Haidian, and Fengtai – which is how the following section is organized. But almost everyone will take a day trip outside Beijing to visit the famous Great Wall, which we discuss at the end of the section.

Dongcheng (East City) District

Once upon a time, Dongcheng District was home to China's emperors. Today in this inner-east section of Beijing, you'll find most of the famous attractions in the historic city. If you are just planning to sightsee in Beijing, staying in East City is a great choice. It's helpful to know that the old city is built on a central north-south axis, on which the most important ancient structures like the Forbidden City and the Drum and Bell Towers are located.

See

Tian'anmen Square
Even those not very familiar with China are likely to have seen Tian'anmen Square and the famous portrait of Chairman Mao hanging on the gate of the square. Tian'anmen Square is one of

the five largest public squares in the world. There are many Soviet-style monuments and government buildings from the early days of the new People's Republic. Aside from the buildings, you can find visitors from around China, many visiting the capital of their country for the first time, as well as many visitors from around the world. At dawn, there is a showy flag raising ceremony, and at dusk, a ceremony to lower the flag, at the northern end of the square.

Transit: Subway Line 2 will take you to Qianmen Station at the southern end of the square, while Subway Line 1 takes you to Tian'anmen East and Tian'anmen West Stations, at the northern end of the square.

In the square you'll find:

Chairman Mao Memorial Hall
Starting at the southern end of the square, the first monument you'll come on is Chairman Mao Memorial Hall, which houses the body of the chairman. Locals disagree as to whether the body is real or a fake waxwork, so you can decide for yourself. Lines are usually long here, but they move very fast. For the devoted, flowers can be purchased to lay at the feet of the Chairman Mao statue outside, which are collected and resold at the end of the day. You can also purchase an informative leaflet for ¥1. Note that bags, cameras, or water bottles are not allowed inside, but must be checked for a small fee at the bag check building across the road to the east. Mobile phones are allowed.

Tian'anmen Gate
Tian'anmen Gate, where the large portrait of Chairman Mao is hung, is one of the most recognizable sights of China. The gate is located on the northern end of the square, and guards the way into the Forbidden City. You can pass through for free, or purchase a ticket on the far side to go up on the gate for a great view over the

entire square. To go into the Forbidden City, you'll need to buy a separate ticket.

Monument to the People's Heroes

This monument at the center of Tian'anmen Square pays homage to key events in modern Chinese history. Consider it as a propaganda poster carved in stone.

Forbidden City (Gu Gong)

Allocate a whole day for this sprawling and spectacular palace complex if you want to truly do it justice. Gates open at 8:30am and close at 5pm. The glittering grandeur of the Chinese court at the height of its power is more apparent here than anywhere else in China. This beautifully preserved city within a city, built as a residence for the emperors, empresses, and the rest of the imperial family of the Ming and Qing dynasties, boasts of many imposing palaces and landscaped courtyards. Every meter is full of history. An unassuming old well might be where one of the emperor's favorite concubines was forced to commit suicide, another might be the meeting spot of a pair of famous forbidden lovers. So be sure to give yourself time to wander and explore. You can rent an audio guided tour that takes you through the history of some of the important buildings along the central axis of the entire complex for ¥40 with a ¥100 deposit. To rest a bit from all the walking, there are a handful of cafes and gift shops that are actually not too overpriced considering the location.

National Museum of China
On the east end of Tian'anmen Square, you can find this world-class museum dedicated to Chinese history. There is an excellent collection of ancient Chinese artifacts, as well as a presentation on modern Chinese history that is, as expected, not entirely objective. It is free to visit and well worth a few hours.

Other sights

Temple of Heaven (Tian Tan)
This beautiful temple was used by the imperial family to make dedications to the gods, pray for good harvests and fair weather

for his people, and carry out other religious ceremonies related to the imperial state. Today, it is an important historical sight surrounded by a vast public park that is the greenest place in Beijing, with many ancient trees, and offers a little peace and solitude in this crowded modern city, especially towards the western gate of the park. In the morning, you'll local residents practicing tai chi, dancing, and exercising in the park.

Transit: Subway Line 5 takes you straight to Tian Tan Dong Men Station (Tian Tan Eastern Gate).

Lama Temple (Yonghe Gong)
Emperors with a deep fascination for Tibetan Buddhism built this temple, and have allowed many renowned Tibetan and Mongolian Buddhist monks to live and teach here. Even today, there are still monks living in and maintaining the temple, most famous for its 18 meters tall statue of Maitreya Buddha, amazingly carved from just a single piece of sandalwood.

Transit: Take Lines 2 or 5 to Yonghe Gong Lama Temple Station.

Drum and Bell Towers (Zhonggu Lou)
The original Drum Tower dates back to 1272, and was reconstructed at its present location straight north from the Forbidden City along the central axis in 1800. The Bell Tower was built around 1700. Originally, the towers were used to announce time similar to church bells in the west. Today, the Bell Tower houses a 63-ton ancient copper bell, while the Drum Tower houses a number of ancient and replica drums. If you make your way up the very steep 60 plus steps of the towers, you'll be rewarded with a spectacular view of the ancient city. Catch a free tour to either tower, or a performance that usually starts at half-past at the Drum Tower.

Transit: Take Subway Line 2 to Gu Lou Avenue.

Experience

Hutong

"Hutong" literally means an alleyway. The name has come to represent the old neighborhoods and traditional way of living of Beijing. While you can find hutong neighborhoods in all four inner districts in Beijing, they are most extensive and best preserved in the East City District. Be sure to wander away from tourist sights and major thoroughfares, especially in the northern half of the district, and you'll be treated to real neighborhoods where the locals - true "old Beijingers" still live, as well as shops, markets, and food stalls that cater to the locals.

The area between Bell Tower and Lama Temple is a good place to start for your exploration. Most lanes run east west and are fairly easy to navigate between those major attractions, which should take about half an hour but of course you'll want to stop, take in the atmosphere, and maybe shop a little. If you don't love walking, fear not - rickshaw drivers can be found in the square between Drum Tower and Bell Tower. Feel free to bargain and shop around to get their prices down.

Nan Luo Gu Xiang

The name of this restored hutong, lined with boutiques and small shops, has become one of the most popular and crowded tourist destinations in Beijing. Just east of Drum Tower, visitors from elsewhere in China and abroad converge here to find interesting and unique gifts like T-shirts with President Obama's picture coupled with a Communist slogan, pottery that mimics imperial styles, and jewelry with a Chinese flair. There are also food stands offering traditional Beijing snacks like a delicious yogurt drink that you drink on the spot from an attractive mason jar. Because it is geared more toward tourists, it can be difficult to find a bargain here; nonetheless, the lively atmosphere is a must for first-time visitors to experience. Note that you might see some partially translated signs that point to "South Luo Gu Alley", that's Nan Luo Gu Xiang!

Transit: Both Line 6 and Line 8 take you to Nan Luo Gu Xiang Station.

Wang Fu Jing

Wang Fu Jing is the most famous shopping district in Beijing, and the commercial heart of the ancient capital. Aside from the same international clothing and electronic brands, you can also find delicious Chinese street food in various stands around the district, including Chinese barbeque. The main street is a pedestrian only street here, allowing you to take a pleasant walk, and have a look at several of the biggest malls in the city, such as Oriental Plaza and Sun Dong An Plaza.

Transit: Take Line 1 to Wang Fu Jing Station.

Xicheng (West City) District

The western part of the inner city of Beijing is the political center of the city, and by extension of course, the political center of China. Several political institutions including central ministries, and residential complexes for the most powerful men and women of the country are located here. For the tourists, there are attractive parks, top museums, and the most famous bar scene in the whole city to visit in this district.

See

Beihai Park

First constructed in the 11th century, Beihai Park was once an imperial garden and caters only to the emperor and his family. Today, many historically important structures, palaces, and temples can be found in this Chinese garden, the largest in the world open to the public. The most recognizable structures in the park are the White Pagoda, which is located in an islet at the center of the park, and the famous Nine-Dragon Wall, built in 1402 and decorated in shimmery glazed bricks in seven colors. Nine vivid dragons play in the clouds on both sides of the wall, each with its own expression. There are two other nine-dragon walls elsewhere in China.

Transit: Take bus 101, 103, 109, or 846 to Beihai South Gate stop, or bus 13, 118, or 810 to Beihai North Gate stop.

Jingshan Park
Built immediately to the north of the Forbidden City around an artificial hill called Jingshan, or "Prospect Hill", this public park used to be a private imperial garden attached to the Forbidden City. The park covers 57 acres - much smaller than Beihai Park, but is just as beautiful. It has been a local favorite for hiking since it opened to the public in 1928.

Transit: Take bus 101, 103, 109, 124, 202, 211, 609, or 685 to Jingshan South, just across Jingshan Front Street from the Forbidden City. Alternatively, take bus 5 or 609 to the east gate of Beihai Park, and walk to the Jingshan West entrance at Jingshan West Street and Doushan Street close by.

Beijing Capital Museum
Established relatively recently in 1981, Beijing Capital Museum already boasts of a massive collection of over 200,000 historical artifacts unearthed in Beijing and around China. Only a small fraction of that collection is exhibited, but there are still more than you can see in a few hours. There are great exhibits that focus on the history of Beijing City. Admission is free.

Transit: Take Subway Line 1 to Muxidi Station.

Beijing Zoo and Aquarium

Many of the rarest animal species in China, including the giant panda, the crested ibis, and the South China tiger, call Beijing Zoo home. Founded in 1906 during the last days of the Qing Dynasty, Beijing Zoo and Aquarium is one of the oldest zoos in the country, and has one of the largest animal collections with over 450 species of land animals and over 500 species of marine animals. More than six million visitors come to the zoo each year to visit the 14,500 animals that live here.

In addition to the animals on exhibit, you can enjoy the beautiful grounds designed to resemble classical Chinese gardens with flower beds, dense tree groves, meadows, meandering small streams, lotus pools and hills dotted with historical temples and pavilions.

Transit: Take Subway Line 4 to Beijing Zoo Station.

Experience

Houhai District

"Back Sea", as the name Houhai literally means, along with "Front Sea" and "Western Sea", make up Shichahai, the collective name for the three northernmost lakes in central Beijing. But since the early 2000s, Houhai has actually come to refer to the neighborhood around Houhai that has become known for its nightlife, especially popular among expats living in Beijing. Many traditional hutong residences along the lakeshore have been converted into some of the most popular bars, restaurants, and cafes in the city. Prices are higher than elsewhere in Beijing, and crowds tend to congregate here, but hanging out with a cold beer and enjoying the view of the lake reflecting the moonlight at night is pretty spectacular.

Transit: Take Subway Line 6 to Beihai North Station.

Xidan District

Xidan is the undisputed shopping mecca of Beijing, and a shopaholic's heaven. There are imposing department stores, popular international brands, as well as bargain shopping options here. There is even a creative underground mall along 77th Street. Locals like to visit bargain malls and - what else - bargain! You'll be more likely to find lower prices here than in the more glittery Wang Fu Jing District. Bargain shoppers should head for Xidan Shopping Center at 132 Xidan North Avenue, while those looking for recognizable international brands can head to the newly built Joy City right next door at 131 Xidan North Avenue.

Transit: Take Subway Line 1 or Line 4 to Xidan Station.

Chaoyang District

A massive district to the north and east of central Beijing, Chaoyang District is a relatively new and less historical area that begins at the Second Ring Road, and stretches beyond the Fifth Ring Road. Most of the new buildings for the 2008 Beijing Olympics can be found in Chaoyang. There is also a thriving art scene, shopping, restaurants, and nightlife in the area.

See

Olympic Green

Many of the venues used for the 2008 Beijing Olympics are in or around the Olympic Green in Chaoyang District. This public square can be visited for free, but you'll need to pay an admission fee for the venues.

Beijing National Stadium, also known as "**Bird's Nest**" for its unique shape, can be found at the Green, and makes for a memorable photo. The stadium was designed by top architecture firm Herzog & Meuron, and currently holds the title of the "World's Largest Steel Structure". During the Olympics, Bird's Nest hosted the opening and closing ceremonies, as well as many athletic matches. There are plans to convert the stadium to a shopping and entertainment complex, since it has found little use after 2008.

Also located in the Olympic Green is the Beijing National Aquatics Center, also known as the Water Cube, which is actually a cuboid - some of its sides are rectangles, not squares. During the 2008 Olympics, swimmers broke 25 world records at the Water Cube, which these days hosts sound and light shows in the evenings.

Transit: Take Subway Line 8 to Olympic Sports Center Station.

Chaoyang Park
This 3 kilometers by 1.5 kilometers park, the largest in Beijing, boasts of an artificial beach, two large swimming pools, a bungee jumping tower, boat rental, convert stages, sports areas, a number of amusement park rides, flower areas, and so much more. Spend

a whole day here, and you still won't be able to see and partake in everything. Locals and tourists alike enjoy taking a stroll here.

Transit: Take Subway Line 10 to Tuanjiehu Station.

798 Art Zone
Built in an old industrial neighborhood of Beijing, 798 Art Zone, cannot be more different from the imposing Olympic buildings and sprawling park grounds that are also located in Chaoyang district. Here you can find the best galleries exhibiting contemporary Chinese art, and tasteful cafes catering to artists and art enthusiasts who frequent the art zone. Even outside the galleries, there is art everywhere - graffiti and paintings on walls, statues, sculptures, and installations in public spaces. You can get a taste of China's contemporary culture as well here, or find unique souvenirs at one of the many shops in the area. You can easily spend half a day or more here and do some people watching for the coolest crowd in Beijing.

Transit: It's located outside Fourth Ring Road, so it's easiest and fastest to get there by taxi. Alternatively, bus routes 688 and 418 go from Dong Zhi Men via Liang Ma Qiao for connections to and from the subway system.

Central Business District (Guo Mao)
The absolute center of Beijing's business world, and the commercial heart of Northern China, Guo Mao features soaring modern architecture and tons of high end shopping. It is also home to Beijing Television Station, and the new China Central Television (CCTV) Headquarters. Explore, shop, or just watch for the beautiful and wealthy here.

Transit: Take Subway Lines 1 or 10 to Guo Mao Station.

Experience

Chaoyang Theater
Forget Cirque du Soleil. You can catch even more impressive acrobatic performances at Chaoyang Theater. There are also Peking Opera performances here, but they are smaller in comparison.

Transit: Take Subway Line 10 to Hu Jia Lou Station.

Pan Jia Yuan Antique Market
Also known as the "dirt market" or the "weekend market" to locals, Pan Jia Yuan is China's largest flea market, and very likely its most entertaining. It is open daily, but most people visit on the weekend, when the market opens from 4am in the morning (7am on weekdays, 8am in the winter). There are tons of antiques - only a small fraction is real, the rest are amusing fakes - as well as a large selection of modern porcelain, jade, carved stone and wood, paintings, furniture, and other interesting finds like Cultural Revolution kitsch that make great souvenirs. Definitely remember to haggle - offer somewhere from 1/10 to ⅓ of the original price, and remember to shop around. Chances are, you'll find the same ware a few stalls down.

Transit: Take Subway Line 10 to Pan Jia Yuan Station.

Silk Street (Yashow)
This five story building sells more than just silk - also luggage, leather bags, electronics, sporting goods, jewelry, clothing, and Chinese artwork. The market caters almost entirely to foreigners these days, and is pretty much a tourist trap with overpriced options. If you buy anything here, be sure to bargain, and bargain hard!

Transit: Take Line 1 to Yong'anli Station.

San Li Tun
The center of expat nightlife in Beijing, San Li Tun has long been one of the top destinations for restaurants, shopping, bars, and of course, night clubs. The crowd here is truly international. The main "bar street" is divided into north and south sections, with a side street with more casual - and cheaper - bars. Since more western style clubs opened elsewhere in Beijing in 2005, San Li Tun has become less cool and more of an institution. You'll have to get past push bar owners and knick-knack vendors as you make your way on the main street. The area is still worth checking out, but the younger party crowd in Beijing is likely to be found in other clubs outside San Li Tun these days. The adjacent Worker's Stadium, or "Gong Ti", area, has also become a nightlife and restaurant hub.

Transit: Tuanjiehu Station on Subway line 10. Take exit A or D.

Haidian District

Haidian District, in northwest Beijing, is home to famous sights like Summer Palace and Fragrant Hills, as well as Tsinghua University and Peking University – the Harvard and Yale of China – and many other top universities.

See

Summer Palace (Yi He Yuan)
As its name implies, Summer Palace was where the Qing Dynasty emperors spent their summers, and includes a vast ensemble of lakes, gardens, and opulent palaces that you can spend hours exploring. These days, the park is both a UNESCO site and a local favorite for recreations. All year long, you can find retirees exercising and dancing here. At the center of the park is

Longevity Hill. On the front, the hill is decorated with splendid halls and palaces, while the back hill, where most tourists do not venture, is quieter and full of natural beauty, with a few secret ruins and caves for you to discover.

Also in the park is Kunming Lake, an entirely manmade lake that covers a massive 540 acres.

Transit: Bei Gong Men Station on Subway Line 4. Take Exit D.

Fragrant Hills (Xiang Shan)
Another of the Qing Dynasty imperial garden, Fragrant Hills is an easy and pleasant climb that on a clear day provides a beautiful view of the ever-expanding Beijing City. World-renowned architect I.M. Pei designed the Fragrant Hills Hotel atop these hills.

Transit: Take buses 331, 360 or 634 to the last stop.

Five Pagoda Temple
"Five Pagoda Temple" refers to the stunning Diamond Throne Tower that is at the heart of the Temple of the Great Righteous Awakening. While the original wooden outer temple was burnt down in 1860 and 1900, the tower, built in brick and marble, survived from the late fifteen century. The temple area is now home to the Beijing Art Museum of Stone Carvings.

Transit: Take Subway Line 4 to National Library Station. Get out of the station from southeast exit (Exit C), walk along Wu Ta Si Road along the Changhe River eastward for 500 meters.

Tsinghua University
One of the recognized top two universities in China along with Peking University, Tsinghua University dates back to 1911, and is the alma mater of many of China's current political leaders and

top intellectuals. Today, the school has developed into essentially a city within a city, as walls separate the campus from the city outside. Part of the school grounds belonged to the old Summer Palace with lots of greens and a lake. There are also grocery stores, banks, post offices, a hospital, and affiliated kindergarten, elementary and middle schools, all catering to those belonging to the university. It is also said to have one of the best dining facilities among Chinese universities. There are close to 20 dining venues, all offering authentic Chinese food for less than ¥10.

Transit: Wu Dao Kou Station of Subway Line 13, and then take Bus Line 549 to Da Shi Qiao stop which is very near to the northeast gate of Tsinghua campus.

Experience

Wu Dao Kou District
A great place to check out youth culture and student nightlife in Beijing, Wu Dao Kou has a great variety of bars and restaurants, most of which are on the cheaper end and cater to the college students from nearby universities. There is also a Korean population in the district, so it's a good place to find authentic Korean food.

Transit: Wu Dao Kou Station of Subway Line 13.

Fengtai District

Marco Polo Bridge (Lu Gou Qiao)

First built in the late 1100s over the Yongding River, Marco Polo Bridge has architectural as well as historical significance. Its western name derives from the famous Venetian traveler Marco Polo, who said in the 13th century that it is a "very fine stone bridge". It is also the site of a clash between Japanese and Chinese forces in 1937, which marked the beginning of the Second Sino-Japanese War.

Transit: Take Subway Line 1 to Wu Ke Song Station. Leave from Exit D1 and take Bus 624 to Kang Zhan Diao Su Yuan (Sculpture Garden) Station.

World Park

It may be an eerie experience to see the large-scale replica of the destroyed World Trade Center Towers here in Beijing, but the World Park, a sort of Las Vegas with its replicas of famous buildings around the world makes for an interesting walk. Fans of Chinese filmmaker Jia Zhangke are probably familiar with the park from Jia's film The World. There are often song-and-dance shows and acrobatic displays here.

Transit: Take Subway Line 1 to Wu Ke Song, and then transfer to bus 967.

Day Trip to the Great Wall of China

One of the most recognizable symbols of China, this magnificent structure, in addition to Beijing, stretches westward across Liaoning, Hebei, Tianjin, Inner Mongolia, Shanxi, Shaanxi, Ningxia, and Gansu provinces in China. The first Great Wall was built during the Qin Dynasty by the first emperor, Shi Huang Di, to guard the country against invaders. The Wall we see today was mostly built during the Ming Dynasty, from 1367 to 1644.

While most visitors take a day trip to it from Beijing, the Great Wall can actually be visited at many places along its several thousand kilometers. The condition of preservation of the Wall ranges from excellent to very rundown, and some sections can be very difficult to reach.

The most popular site from Beijing is Ba Da Ling, a very well restored and maintained section of the Wall. It can be very crowded on the weekends, so aim for a weekday if you can.

Ba Da Ling

Getting There:

By Subway and Bus

Take Subway Line 2 to Ji Shui Tan Station. Once you get out of the station, walk east on the north side of the road to the bus station, and catch Bus 877, which takes you to the front hill of Ba Da Ling in around an hour. From there, it takes about 10 minutes to walk to the ticket office of the Great Wall.

The last Bus 877 leaves from Beijing at around 12:30pm, while the last bus from Ba Da Ling leaves around 4:30pm. Since many visitors flock to the Great Wall, get to the bus stop early if you want a seat for the one hour long bus ride.

By Train

A train runs from Beijing North Railway Station to Ba Da Ling Railway Station, and takes around one hour and 20 minutes. From there, it takes about 15 to 20 minutes to the entrance of the Great Wall.

Day Tour
A day tour to Ba Da Ling costs around 170 to 250 RMB. Don't get ripped off, as many tour companies will try to charge double for foreigners.

Walking and Hiking
Even though the wall is paved, you should prepare as you would for a hike – wear comfortable clothes you can move in and proper hiking shoes, and add plenty of layers if you are visiting during the colder months. Expect a lot of hills and very steep steps.

At the entrance to Ba Da Ling, you'll usually see large crowds, but as you hike further on, you'll see less and less people. It takes around two to three hours to hike the entire stretch of the wall at Ba Da Ling, depending on your fitness.

Those who have mobility difficulties should take the cable car in front of the entrance for 85 RMB.

Other Sections of the Wall

Mu Tian Yu
The lesser-known Mu Tian Yu is further away from Beijing compared to Ba Da Ling, but is just well restored and much less crowded. The surrounding hills are also greener and more scenic than Ba Da Ling. Even better, the large tour groups do not go here, so you have the luxury of a less hectic Great Wall experience. There is a ski lift to get on and off the Wall, or you

can take a toboggan ride down. You have to take a cab to reach Mu Tian Yu.

Huang Hua Cheng

This section of Ming Dynasty Wall is one of the most well built sections. It is located at Jiu Du He town, about 40 miles from Beijing. The entire section is about 6.7 miles long, complete with mountains and lakes that complement the Wall. In the summer, the entire area is covered in a sea of yellow wild flowers that make for a very beautiful day trip. A special tourist bus runs from Dong Zhi Men Transportation Hub in Beijing to Huang Hua Cheng on Saturday, Monday, and legal holidays. Otherwise, it is easiest to drive or take a cab.

Eat

As in any metropolitan cities, in Beijing you can find virtually any type of cuisine you crave. Still, from the famous Peking Duck, to the more strange looking boiled lamb tripe, the capital city of China is famous for a huge range of food native to its ancient city limits.

Peking Roast Duck (Beijing Kao Ya)

The name says it all – if there is one dish that is Beijing to the core, it's Peking duck. A succulent whole roast duck is sliced into decadent pieces of crispy skin and tender meat. The dish is served with pancakes, cucumber, green onion, and a sweet paste. You assemble everything into a small burrito and bite!

There are restaurants all over Beijing serving this classic dish. The classic restaurant synonymous with Peking duck is "Quan Ju De," with three flagship branches in the city. In particular, the location around Qian Men is the most interesting with beautiful views of the ancient city and special presentation of the duck – your food served with a dollop of culture. Expect to pay around ¥150-200 per person.

Mutton Hot Pot (Shuan Yang Rou)

Those from the U.S. may be familiar with a version of hot pot with a spicy broth and a white broth. The hot pot in Beijing is a different and – in many locals' opinion – more delicious variety. Paper-thin slices of mutton is dipped into a piping hot pot of broth and cooked instantly. You then dip the meat in a special sauce of sesame, bean curd, and green onions. This is such a treat in the harsh winters of Beijing.

Among the many hot pot restaurants, Dong Lai Shun is a favorite with locals and tourists alike, for about ¥150 per person. Fu Man

Lou is also good, and instead of one large pot that everyone dips into, you get your own cute individual pot for around ¥100.

Zha Jiang Noodles (Zha Jiang Mian)

This cheap and delicious dish is very popular in Beijing and northern China. Hand-pulled noodles are topped with a savory bean sauce, shredded cucumber and pickled radishes. You can find them in every little hole-in-the-wall place in Beijing.

Boiled Lamb Tripe (Bao Du)

Don't let the name put you off – when done correctly, this Islamic snack tastes amazing. Pieces of fresh lamb tripe are quickly cooked in boiling water, and served with a delicious dipping sauce of sesame sauce, vinegar, chili oil, and green onions.

Jin Sheng Long in Haidian District has been specializing in Bao Du for over 100 years. Qing Dynasty aristocrats loved the place, so you'll be in good company.

Another classic with just as many years of history, Bao Du Feng, offers a bunch of different lamb parts, cooked in different ways. They are all delicious, especially when dipped into Bao Du Feng's secret sauce.

Street Snacks

Some of Beijing's best food can be found right on the street. You can sample an extremely big selection of everything from classic Beijing baked goods to novelties like fried scorpions. Let your eyes, nose, and stomach guide you.

The earliest Beijing snack street is Gui Jie, or Ghost Street. The 1.5-kilometer-long street is always open, but most people frequent between 6pm and 4am.

Wang Fu Jing Snack Street is close to the famous shopping district of the same name. Tourists discovered this gem quite a while ago, so expect to rub elbows with locals as well as fellow travelers while you snack on lamb kebabs or candied fruits. There are also some souvenir stalls here.

Breakfast Snacks

Come out of your hotel in the morning, and you'll likely see busy office workers lining up in front of stalls selling a variety of classic Beijing breakfasts. You can try fried dough (**Jiao Quan**) with soymilk, or street crepe (**Jian Bing Guo Zi**). There are also stalls specializing in buns filled with sweet beans or meat, and many others. If you see locals eating something, it's probably good and very cheap.

Getting In and Out

By Air
Most travelers, foreign and domestic, will fly into Beijing Capital International Airport. Alternatively, you can consider flying into Tianjin Binhai International Airport, which mainly serves the first-tier city of Tianjin, and is just 35 minutes away from Beijing by express train.

From Beijing Airport, you can take the Airport Express train, which runs in between terminals 3 and 2, then into the city. You can connect to Subway Line 1 at San Yuan Qiao Station, or Lines 2 and 13 at Dong Zhi Men Station. The ticket is ¥25 for one way, and takes about 20 minutes from T2 to Dong Zhi Men, or 30 minutes from T3.

Alternatively, a taxi takes you into the city for ¥70-120. Join the taxi queue, avoid going with the drivers offering to take you elsewhere near the airport. It would help a lot to get the Chinese name of your hotel written in characters.

By Train
The train network is extensive and well developed across China. However, note that during national holidays and peak travel periods, it is a good idea to book train tickets well in advance of your planned travel dates, as they sell out fast with everyone trying to get to their hometown or to tourist destinations. Most train ticket sales open 10 to 21 days in advance.

There are generally four classes of train tickets in China. Soft sleeper class, where four bunks are isolated in each "room"; hard sleeper class, which is a bit less comfortable with six bunks to each section, exposed to the aisle; hard seating, which is little more than a covered wooden bench, and the plusher soft seat. If you choose to purchase a seating ticket for a bargain price, remember that you'll likely be surrounded by smokers, loud noise, and people playing cards in a crowded compartment, especially in hard seating. For longer trips, it is advisable to choose a sleeper ticket.

There are three major train stations – Central, West, and South – in Beijing, which will have trains to and from most of the major tourist destinations around China. There is also a smaller North Station that you'll likely not use.

Beijing Central Railway Station (Beijing Zhan)
Central Station is in the heart of the city, served by Subway Line 2. You can reach major tourist destinations around China including Hangzhou, Suzhou, and Shanghai, as well as other major cities like Changchun, Chengde, Dalian, Fuzhou, Guangzhou, Harbin, Nanjing, Shenyang, Tianjin, Qiqihar, and Yangzhou.

Beijing West Railway Station (Beijing Xi Zhan)
High-speed trains to and from Xi'an, as well as regular trains to and from Chengdu, Hong Kong, Guilin, and Lhasa arrive at West Station. There are also high-speed trains to and from major cities including Shijiazhuang, Taiyuan, Zhengzhou, Wuhan, Changsha, Guangzhou, and Shenzhen, and regular trains from Changsha, Chongqing, Datong, Fuzhou, Guiyang, Hohhot, Kunming, Lanzhou, Ningbo, Qinhuangdao, Sanya, Urumqi, and Xiamen.

Beijing South Railway Station (Beijing Nan Zhan)
High-speed services run daily to and from Shanghai and Hangzhou from South Station. There are also trains to Tianjin, Tanggu, Jinan, Qingdao, Nanjing, Fuzhou, and other destinations.

Getting Around in Beijing

The Beijing Subway system is extensive and a great way to quickly get around. All signs are in Chinese as well as English for international travelers. It is generally a more economical mode of transportation compared to taxies, and more convenient compared to the buses.

Depending on the distance, a subway ride should cost between ¥3-9. There is no weekly or monthly passes currently, but you can get an "Yi Ka Tong", a pre-paid card with a ¥20 refundable deposit and never expires, to avoid the often long lines of purchasing a new ticket for every ride. You can refill and add value to this card as you need.

Xi'an

Introduction

Xi'an is the capital of the Shaanxi Province, which is considered the cradle of ancient Chinese culture. The city of Xi'an, or Chang'an as it was known then, with more than 3,000 years of history, was the capital city of 13 dynasties and home to 73 emperors, starting from the Zhou Dynasty dating back to 1046 BC.

The ancient city was also the starting point of the Silk Road. Traders from as far as Ancient Rome brought goods and ideas to Xi'an, and took away Chinese goods and ideas back to their native land. Unfortunately, constant wars in recent centuries have destroyed much of the city's heritage, but the city remains one of the most popular tourist destinations in China, if for the famous Terracotta Warriors alone.

See

Inside the City

City Wall of Xi'an (Cheng Qiang)

The ancient city wall of Xi'an is the largest in the world, having been restored to 12 meters high, 18 meters wide at its base, 15 meters wide on the top, and 13.7 kilometers long. Like most sections of the Great Wall, the Xi'an city walls you see today were mostly built during the Ming Dynasty from the 14th to the 17th century. However, the foundations date back to the Imperial City – called Chang'an in those days – during the Tang Dynasty from the 7th to the 10th century.

There are eight points of entry to the walls around the perimeter. The walls are lit by theatrical lights at night, and make for a very pleasant after supper stroll. You can also rent a bike at the four main gates for 120 minutes at ¥45 per person, and ride along the top of the walls. Sometimes you can catch traditional Chinese performances along the walls.

There is also a landscaped park around the base of the exterior walls and moat that is also nice to walk through, and offers a different view of the battlements and towers from below.

Shaanxi History Museum

The province of Shaanxi, where Xi'an is located, has been inhabited since the Neolithic Age. The Shaanxi History Museum pays homage to the region's long history, and houses a collection of local artifacts from the Neolithic Age through the Qing Dynasty. Archaeology enthusiasts will want to see the very well preserved pottery from the nearby Ban Po Neolithic Village that are some of the oldest in the world, as well as intricate bronze artifacts from the Shang Dynasty.

Transit: Take Bus No. 5, 19, 24, 26, 27, 30, 34, 400 or Tourist Bus No. 8 (610) and get off at Cuihua Road bus stop.

Forest of Stone Steles Museums

Over 2,300 stone tablets and epitaphs make up this forest, the largest and oldest of its kind in China, and a huge "official" source of Chinese historical and literary classics that might otherwise have been lost. Be sure to look for the Nestorian Stele, which dates back to the 7th century and depicts the arrival of Nestorian Christianity in China.

Transit: Take tourism bus no.6 or Take bus no.14, 23, 40, 208, and get off at Wen Chang Gate Station.

Big Wild Goose Pagoda (Da Yan Ta)

A famous emblem of the ancient capital and lauded in many of the most well-known poems by famous Chinese poets, the Big Wild Goose Pagoda was built in 652AD by a Tang Dynasty emperor, originally to store Buddhist sutras and other artifacts brought from India by the Buddhist monk and traveler Xuan Zang. Successive natural disasters destroyed the structure numerous times. The current pagoda was extensively repaired and rebuilt in the Ming Dynasty. There is also a Small Wild Goose Pagoda in Xi'an.

There is a tranquil fountain in front of the pagoda, where water and music shows take place throughout the day. You can also find pleasant parks and western eateries catering to tourists around here.

Transit: Take Subway Line 2 to Xiao Zhai Station. Take Exit C, and walk east for 10 minutes.

Great Mosque
This grand mosque, the very first built in China, is today the largest, and best-preserved Islamic mosque in China. It is built in mixed Islamic and Chinese architectural styles, and can accommodate 1,000 worshipers at a time.

A Muslim Street District, with many winding backstreets, has developed around the mosque. It is still used as a place of worship, so only Muslims are permitted entry to the actual mosque building. However, there is a lot to see in the many courtyards that surround the mosque. Per the Muslim tradition, women are asked to cover their heads with scarves prior to entering the grounds.

Transit: Take bus Take bus 4, 7, 32, 201, 215, 222 or Tourism Bus No. 8 (610) and get off at Zhong Lou Station.

Tang Paradise (Da Tang Fu Rong Yuan)
Built just to the north of the original Tang Dynasty Lotus Garden, Tang Paradise is actually a theme park designed to reconstruct the grandeur of the royal garden in its heyday during the Tang Dynasty. The park set many impressive records, including the largest movie on water screen in the world, the first theme park that appeals to all five senses, and biggest outdoor fragrant project in the world, and the biggest reproduction of Tang Dynasty royal garden complexes in China.

Transit: Take Bus 21, 22, 23, 24, 44, 212 and get off at Da Tang Fu Rong Yuan Station or Da Tang Fu Rong Yuan Nan Men Station.

Outside the City

Terracotta Warriors and Horses

These ancient terracotta soldiers and horses are the most popular attraction of Xi'an with over 2 million visitors per year, and have become one of the symbols of China. Qin Shi Huang, the first emperor of the Qin Dynasty and in Chinese history, assembled this enormous army of around 8,000 to protect him in the afterlife.

On display in the in-site museum covering a total of 20,000 square meters, you can see 2,000 intricately sculpted terracotta warriors, 100 terracotta chariots, and 30,000 weapons. These are not cheap knockoffs either – take the time to look at the warriors closely, and you'll notice each sports different hairstyles and clothes according to his rank and function, different facial expressions, and even palm lines. Imagine how long this must have taken Qin artisans. The site is so impressive that the tourist industry has billed it as the Eighth Wonder of the World. It has been a UNESCO World Cultural Heritage Site since 1987.

After looking at the warriors, you can visit the nearby Qin Shi Huang Mausoleum, which is a large park and a good place to rest for a while. It is free to visit with a ticket to the Terracotta Warriors.

Transit: From the main train station in Xi'an, take bus 306, 914, or 915. There are always a lot of tourists going to the same place, so you won't miss it. Journey time is approximately 80 minutes.

Mount Hua (Hua Shan)
Located 120 kilometers east of the city of Xi'an, Mount Hua is one of the five Great Mountains of China, and one of its most sacred. There are five peaks, the highest being the South Peak at 2,154.9 meters.

Mount Hua has long been home to many temples and other religious structures throughout China's long history. At the foot of the mountain is the tranquil Cloister of the Jade Spring, while at the top of the South Peak there is an ancient Taoist temple that has been converted to a nice teahouse today.

Transit: There is a high-speed train from Xi'an that takes you to Mount Hua in around 40 minutes. Alternatively, you can take the tourism bus No. 5(306). Once at the Hua Shan Train Station, you can take a quick cab to the mountain trailhead. There is also a cable car that can take you to the top. The peaks can be explored in 3 to 4 hours from where the cable car drops off.

Hua Qing Hot Springs
Built by a Tang emperor at the foot of Mt. Li, just 30 kilometers outside Xi'an City, Hua Qing Hot Springs were meant to be a getaway for the emperor and his favorite imperial concubine, Lady Yang. The lady was reputedly one of the four most beautiful women in Chinese history, and bewitched the emperor until the country broke out in revolts.

Today, you can bath in the imperial style among the hot spring's scenic surroundings, and imagine yourself back in the height of the opulent Tang Dynasty. The garden grounds are quite beautiful as well, and are ranked among the 100 Famous Gardens in China.

Transit: From the Xi'an Railway Station, take tourism bus No. 5 (306) toward the Terracotta Warriors. Get off at the Hua Qing Chi Stop.

Experience

Muslim Quarter (Hui Min Jie)
This district around the Great Mosque is a fun place to wander and get some cheap Islamic-Chinese food, including local favorites like roast beef, roast fish, and a special pancake. Peruse the stalls along the winding alleyways, and you'll likely find very cheap and unique souvenirs to take home. As in all street markets in China, don't forget to bargain.

Transit: Take bus Take bus 4, 7, 32, 201, 215, 222 or Tourism Bus No. 8 (610) and get off at Zhong Lou Station.

Eat

Xi'an and Shaanxi Province in general, are known for their noodles, buns, and other wheat-based foods. Everything is more or less homemade and more delicious as a result. We highlight a few varieties below, but you should try as many as you can while in Xi'an.

Pita Bread Soaked in Lamb Soup (Yang Rou Pao Mo)
This is a dish as famous as it is ancient. You are served a delicious mutton stew, into which you break pita bread, which makes the stew even heartier. Locals eat it year-round, but there is nothing like slurping down a big bowl of this when it's cold outside.

Pork Burger (Rou Jia Mo)
No, the Chinese didn't steal this from McDonald's. This popular local snack is made with tender pork, stewed for hours and in a flavorful sauce with over 20 kinds of local spices, sandwiched between pita bread. For around ¥5-10, you get a filling and delicious meal out of pork burger.

Cold Skin Noodles (Liang Pi)
There are many variations on this, but the classic is a chewy and semi-transparent thick noodle made from rice, dressed in a spicy sauce, served with bean sprouts, cucumber, and cilantro. It is a very invigorating taste in every season.

Food Streets
As with other Chinese cities, Xi'an has a vibrant street food scene. The Muslim Quarter has cheap, authentic, Islamic food with a Chinese twist, while Dongxin Street Night Market offers dishes from Xi'an and elsewhere in China.

Getting In and Out

By Air
Xi'an Xianyang International Airport (XIY) is about 25 miles outside the city center, in the town of Xianyang. Domestic flights are available to most cities in China, and take no more than 2 hours since Xi'an is located in the heart of China. International flights are also available from Helsinki, Bangkok, Hong Kong, Macau, Seoul, Singapore, and many Japanese cities.

To and From the Airport
You can take a taxi from the airport, however this is quite expensive at around ¥150, and drivers will likely take advantage of foreigners and hike the price. In addition to the regular green taxies, you'll see the climatized Japanese-brand black cabs waiting outside the airport as well, these will run ¥50-75 in addition to the regular cab fare.

The airport bus is a better way to reach city center. There are six routes, each running every half hour between 6am and 6pm. You can purchase a ticket at the counter inside the arrival terminal. The ticket is ¥26, and takes at least an hour. The most useful is Airport Bus No.2, which goes to the railway station, and No.1, which runs to the periphery of Old Town.

By Train
Xi'an Station is located on Jie Fang Road, just outside the northeast city wall. Many bus lines take you directly to the station.

Most major cities in China are connected to Xi'an by train. However, as anywhere in China, buy your tickets well ahead of planned travel time. Trains to Beijing take anywhere from 5 to 13 hours, Chengdu from 13 to 18 hours, Lhasa in 36 hours, and Shanghai in 11 to 20 hours.

Getting Around in Xi'an

Subway
The subway system in Xi'an is still being developed. There are only three lines in operation at the present. Line 1 runs north-south to and from Xi'an North Train Station. Line 2 runs east-west and crosses Line 1 in the middle of the city. Line 3 runs in the northeast0southwest direction, and intersects with Line 1 and 2.

Bus
The bus system is quite convenient and extensive, and will take you to most sights with the city. The Tourism Office Center, near the Bell Tower, offers a free map of the city listing all the bus lines and stops. This is very helpful.

Line #610 is popular among tourists to Xi'an. It is also labeled "You 8", which means "Tourist #8 in Chinese. It runs from the railway station, to the top sights: Bell Tower, Small Goose Pagoda, Xi'an Museum, Shaanxi Historic Museum, and Big Goose Pagoda.

CENTRAL CHINA

Suzhou

The city of Suzhou is as beautiful as a classical Chinese painting, with ample water running through the city, and stunningly arranged classical gardens that line the canals. In 1997, the classical gardens were inscribed on the UNESCO World Heritage List.

This ancient city dates back to the Kingdom of Wu, from the 12th to the 4th century BC, before even the time of the first emperor of China. After the kingdom was conquered, the city continued to be the center of the Wu culture, which flourished in these parts.

Today, Suzhou is a core city of the Yangtze River Delta Economic Zone. It is an epicenter of China's silk production and trade as it was in ancient China, and its beautiful canals and tranquil gardens continue to inspire scholars, artists, craftsmen, and travelers every day.

A rectangular canal known as the Weichang River, or Weichang He in Chinese binds downtown Suzhou, composed of Canglang, Pingjiang, and part of Jinchang Districts. Most of the major tourist destinations are within its limits.

See

Suzhou's Classical Chinese Gardens
Suzhou is renowned worldwide for its classical Chinese gardens that are each like a piece of art. Aristocrats and other wealthy businessmen have been building these delicate private residences since the 6th century BC, but their designs underwent a particularly artful phase during the Ming Dynasty, from the 14th to the 17th century. In the subsequent Qing Dynasty, these gardens became more prevalent, spreading across the city and its suburbs.

At its core, the architectural philosophy of these gardens strives to recreate nature on a miniature scale. Therefore, the residential part of the garden exists in beautiful harmony with the ponds, rockeries, flowers, and trees, all designed to exhibit Chinese philosophy and ideology. Each small plot of land is carefully curated to evoke grander locales, like mountains and natural springs. Shielded from the bustling city outside by high walls, these gardens are meant to be tranquil havens for their masters, and evoke for visitors today the forgotten elegance of the old China.

Many of these gardens have been restored close to their former glory. The following are the most famous and popular ones in Suzhou.

The Humble Administrator's Garden (Zhuo Zheng Yuan)

Zhuo Zheng Yuan, covering about 12.85 acres, is the largest of the preserved gardens in Suzhou. If you only visit one garden in Suzhou, this would be the one. The garden is renowned for its unique designs and ethereal beauty, and has garnered many honors, including a World Cultural Heritage Site, a Cultural Relic of National Importance under the Protection of the State, and a Special Tourist Attraction of China. It is also considered one of the four most famous gardens in China.

Though its name nods to its master's aspiration to remain a humble servant of the emperor, this garden is anything but humble. Originally built in 1509, during the Ming Dynasty, it took over 16 years to construct, and was said to have cost a boatload of silver to complete.

Transit: Take bus no. 40 or 313, and get off at Bei Yuan Lu Station.

The Garden of the Master of the Nets (Wang Shi Yuan)
A small but infinitely intricate complex, the Garden of the Master of the Nets dates back to 1140 in the Song Dynasty, and was recreated in 1770. Even though it is the smallest of the preserved gardens in Suzhou, you can easily spend half a day or more here, since the artful use of space creates the illusion that the space is much larger than its actual size. On some evenings, you can catch a traditional performance here.

Transit: take bus no. 55, 202, 529, 811 or 931 and get off at Wang Shi Yuan Station

The Lingering Garden (Liu Yuan)
Considered one of the four most famous gardens in China along with the Humble Administrator's Garden, the Lingering Garden is a prominent example of the Qing Dynasty aesthetic, and one of the most stunning classical gardens in Suzhou. It covers 5.8 acres

outside the original city gate, and is known for its magnificent halls with a range of splendid colors. It became a UNESCO World Heritage Site in 1997.

Transit: Take bus no. 34, 44, 45, 85, 161, 311, 406, 933, 949, or Tourism Bus No. 1 to Liu Yuan Station.

The Lion Grove Garden (Shi Zi Lin)
More than other gardens in Suzhou, the Lion Grove Garden is renowned for its array of pitted, eroded rocks that are beautifully arranged, almost like natural, large-scale sculptures. Together, these rocks used to be part of a Buddhist monastery, and in the garden make up a small maze with many twists and turns that children will enjoy exploring.

Transit: Take bus no. 529, 811 or Tourism Bus No.1, 2, & 5, to Suzhou Museum Station.

Suzhou Museum
The Suzhou Museum contains over 15,000 artifacts, including many prized ancient calligraphy, paintings, and other artifacts unearthed in Suzhou and nearby areas. In particular, the porcelain bowls are stunningly restored, and the splendid antique Chinese gowns will make any modern fashionista envious with their luxurious fabrics and intricate craftsmanship.

World-renowned architect, I.M. Pei, who also designed the glass pyramid outside the Louvre in Paris, among many other works across the U.S, specially designed the building. While Pei lived in America for most of his life, his family actually came from Suzhou. To pay respect to his hometown, Pei came out of retirement in his 80s to create this museum that showcases both his modernist sensibility, and the architectural influence and sophisticated taste of this region. The recreated scholar's study is a highlight of the museum.

The museum is free to visit.

Transit: Take bus no. 529, 811 or Tourism Bus No.1, 2, & 5, to Suzhou Museum Station.

Tiger Hill and Tiger Hill Pagoda
The hill, also known as Surging Sea Hill, covers just over three acres of land, and is 118 feet in height. Though the area is relatively small, it is rich in interesting historical sites that date all the way back to the founding of Suzhou, over 2,500 years ago.

The most famous of the Tiger Hill sites is the Tiger Hill Pagoda, which stands at the summit of the hill, as a part of the Yun Yan Temple. It is the oldest pagoda in Suzhou and the surrounding areas, dating back to the Northern Song Dynasty in the 10th century. It has become known as the "Leaning Tower of China", for its incline similar to the Leaning Tower of Pisa in Italy. Its seven-story octahedron shape, measuring over 150 feet high, is constructed in the style of the timber pagodas characteristic of the early Tang Dynasty.

Transit: Take bus no. 32 or express line 3 and get off at Hu Qiu Bei Men (North Gate of Tiger Hill).

Cold Mountain Temple (Hanshan Temple)
In A Night Mooring near Maple Bridge, a famous Tang Dynasty poem, the poet Zhang Ji describes the midnight bells of the Hanshan Temple, and evokes beautifully the tranquil ancient surroundings of the temple. Since then, the temple has become a popular tourist destination even in ancient China, renowned for its bells and the Buddhist culture. The temple was originally constructed in the Liang Dynasty, in the 6th century, but most of the buildings you see today date from the Tang Dynasty in the 7th century.

Maple Bridge, or Feng Qiao, as described in the poem, is located next to the temple. There is also a statue of the poet nearby, as well as shops selling souvenirs related to both the temple and the bridge.

Transit: Take the special Tourism Bus No.3 (You3 Bus) to Lai Feng Qiao.

Experience

Shan Tang Street

This recently-restored canal street runs from Chang Men, the ancient city gate, to Tiger Hill. It winds along the Shan Tang River for about 2.2 miles or seven "li" – seven Chinese miles, hence the nickname "Seven-Li Shan Tang". The pedestrian street offers a nice stroll, with local snack and souvenir vendors along both sides. While the southeast end of the street close to the city gates may be crowded with tourists, stalls, and touristy restaurants, the northern end is quieter and much nicer for a leisurely walk. It also passes through some local residential neighborhoods, so you'll have a chance to glimpse into how the locals live.

You can also take a river cruise at various points along the walk, to experience the city from the water.

Transit: Take Subway Line 2 to Shantang Street Station.

Eat

Suzhou is known for its fish dishes, made with fresh fish from the lake, cooked more delicately compared to in northern China. In particular, try "**Squirrel-Shaped Fish**", or Song Shu Yu, which is a lightly fried whole deboned fish, dressed in a sweet and sour sauce, or **Whitebait Soup**, which is made with a small, smooth fish, bamboo shoots, and vegetables. Other dishes in traditional Suzhou cuisine are just as carefully prepared. Expect subtle but nuanced flavors.

Getting In and Out

By Air
Suzhou does not have its own commercial airport. Most travelers fly into Shanghai, and travel by train to Suzhou. The airport in the city of Wuxi is closer, but serves mostly domestic flights. Nanjing and Hangzhou are other options.

By Train
Suzhou Station (Suzhou Zhan)
Just north of downtown, Suzhou Station is a stop on the Shanghai-Nanjing train line. There are frequent high-speed connections to Shanghai, Wuxi, Changzhou, Zhenjiang, and Nanjing. A high-speed "G-train" takes you to Shanghai in less than half an hour, and Nanjing in an hour. There are also slower T- and K- trains at this station to and from other provinces.

Suzhou North Railway Station (Suzhou Bei Zhan)
This station, located on the outskirts of the city, serves high-speed trains to and from Beijing, which only takes about five hours.

By Bus
Three inter-city bus terminals in Suzhou offer regular shuttles to Shanghai, Nanjing, Hangzhou, and other major destinations around China.

Getting Around in Suzhou

Subway
The one functioning subway line runs east west between New District, Old Town, and Suzhou Industrial Park. A second line is under construction.

Bus
The extensive bus lines cover the entire city, and run at 10 to 20 minute internals between 5am and 9pm on most routes. They are

quite affordable. All information and announcements are in Chinese only, but you can search on Google Maps ahead of time to plan your travel.

Hangzhou

The city of Hangzhou, located at the southern terminus of the Grand Canal and on the lower reaches of the Qiantang River, was the capital city of the Southern Song Dynasty from 1127, until Mongols overran it in 1276. At the time, with as many as one million inhabitants, Hangzhou was the largest city in the world, and so grand that Marco Polo called it "beyond dispute the finest and the noblest in the world".

Today, Hangzhou is one of the most popular tourist destinations in China. Its subtropical monsoon climate makes the city variedly beautiful in each season. As such, the West Lake, the city's most renowned landmark, has been lauded throughout history for its scenes in different seasons.

See

West Lake Area

West Lake (Xi Hu)
The beauty of the West Lake has inspired poets, artists, and lovers throughout Chinese history. This most scenic and famous of lakes in Hangzhou is surrounded by mountains on three sides, and divided into five inner lakes – the North Inner Lake, the Yuehu Lake, the West Inner Lake, the South Lake, and the West Outer Lake by the three causeways named after famous Chinese poets – the Bai Causeway, the Su Causeway, and the Yang Causeway. There are several large natural islands, as well as a few man-made islands that dot the vast lake district.

During the Qing Dynasty, Emperor Kangxi, who visited West Lake a few times, came up with 10 Scenes of the West Lake – 10 most scenic spots of the area in a season during which it is most beautiful, like "Snowfall over Broken Bridge." He later added 10 more called 10 New Scenes of the West Lake. We highlight a few of the top scenes below.

Transit: Take Subway Line 1 to Long Xiang Qiao. Upon arrival, walk westward to reach the Lakeside Park (Music Fountain) or northward to Broken Bridge or Bai Causeway.

Alternatively, take the same subway to Ding'an Road. Upon arrival, walk westward to lakeside Nanshan Mountain area or southward to Wushan Mountain area.

Dawn on the Su Causeway in Spring
Constructed under the guidance of and named after the great Song Dynasty poet Su Dongpo, the Su Causeway stretches over 1.7 miles, and includes six beautiful bridges along its length: the Crossing Rainbow Bridge, the Eastern lakeside Bridge, the Suppressing Dike Bridge, the Viewing Hills Bridge, the Locking Waves Bridge, and the Reflecting Ripples Bridge. As the name of the scene suggests, this causeway is most breathtaking in the spring, when the willow trees that line its entirety become a fresh green, and the peach trees bear pink blossoms. At dawn, everything is bathed in gold. It is quite worth getting up in the dark if you are up for it.

Winery Yard and Lotus Pool in Summer
In the Southern Song Dynasty, there was a winery at this spot in the northwest section of the lake that in the summer would be surrounded by lotus flowers in the lake around it. The intoxicating aroma of wine mixed with the fragrance of lotus flowers and together, carried by the gentle lakeside breeze, reached unsuspecting visitors for miles.

There is much to be appreciated at a single scenic spot here, including Yuehu Lake, the Bamboo Garden, the Lakeside Woods, the Winery Yard, and the Lotus Pool. You can sample imperial wine while looking over the stunning summer lotus flowers, or take a walk through the beautiful gardens characteristic of southern China.

Lingering Snow on the Broken Bridge in Winter
The famous Broken Bridge is actually famously not broken. Situated at the foot of the Precious Stone Hill to the eastern end of the Bai Causeway, the bridge is named for the view of it from the hill after snow: snow in the middle section of the bridge melts first, while snow at either ends linger a while longer, causing the illusion that the bridge is broken in the middle. The remaining white snow glistens in the sunshine.

Moon over the Peaceful Lake in Autumn
For the traditional Chinese Mid-Autumn Festival, there is no better place to appreciate the glorious full moon than the West Lake, specifically at the Peaceful Lake to the west of the Bai Causeway. There is an octagonal pavilion at the spot, a platform over the lake, and some other buildings, all constructed for admiring the full moon. Chinese literary luminaries over the ages have left their tributes to the same full moon, which can now be seen in the Xi Ling Calligraphy and Painting Gallery, also at this spot.

Lei Feng Pagoda in Evening Glow
The famous pagoda, standing on the Lei Feng Peak of the Sunset Hill to the south of the West Lake, is the first colorful branze pagoda in China. The top of the pagoda offers a stunning view of the nearby Jing Ci Temple, the landscapes of the West Lake, and even the city of Hangzhou in the distance. In the evening, the late sun casts its golden lights on the colorful pagoda and the green mountains, both reflected in the rippling lake.

Other Areas in Hangzhou

Temple of Soul's Retreat (Ling Yin Temple)
There are two peaks to the northwest of the West Lake – Peak Flown from Afar, and North Peak. In the narrow valley between

them is the Temple of Soul's Retreat, one of the three oldest and most famous temples in China. The monastery dates back to 328 AD, during the Eastern Jin Dynasty. Its founder is a legendary monk from India known as Hui Li.

Aside from the temple, there are a large number of grottos and religious rock carvings that are worth admiring. All together, there are hundreds of Buddhist stone statues carved directly into these cliffs.

Transit: Take Tourism Bus No. 1 (Y1), Tourism Bus No. 2 (Y2), 7/K7, Y13, K807/K837 to Ling Yin Temple Station.

Six Harmonies Pagoda (Liu He Pagoda)
This stunning masterpiece of ancient Chinese architecture sits atop Yue Lun Hill, overlooking Qian Tang River and the southern tip of the West Lake. The pagoda is octagonal in shape, and appears to have 13 stories when seen from the outside. Interestingly though, on the inside, there are only seven stories. You can count them! A spiral staircase leads to the top of the pagoda. Each story has an elaborate carved and painted ceiling made up of animals, flowers, birds, and characters from Chinese myths.

After climbing the pagoda, head to the nearby park where you can find hundreds of models of the world's most famous pagodas, complete with miniature trees to scale.

Transit: Take K808, K599, 504, Tourism Bus No. 5 to Liu He Pagoda.

Experience

He Fang Ancient Street (He Fang Jie)

This ancient street allows you to experience the historical and cultural character of Hangzhou firsthand. You can find an amazing array of interesting storefronts along its length, including shops showcasing a variety of Chinese crafts like hand-blown sugar candy, paper-cutting, and hand-made dough figurines, and vendors selling local snacks like roasted walnuts and "dragon-whisker" candy. There are also art hawkers, fabric shops, caricaturists, bonsai shops, teahouses and many small eateries.

Walk around the West Lake
The entire lake would take about five hours to walk around at a leisurely pace. The causeways cut through it if you feel like taking a short cut. There are also small non-motor powered boats you can hire for ¥120/hour to take you around the lake and the two main islands.

Spend an Afternoon at a Tea House.

Hangzhou is famous for its production of Long Jing, the most famous green tea in China, so be sure to find a teahouse and sample some locally grown teas while you are here. You can also visit nearby villages known for their tea farms – Man Jue Long Village, Long Jing Village, or Mei Jia Wu Village. They have been developed for tourism over the last two or three years, and can be quite crowded on the weekends with tourists, but during the week or the offseason, you can still spend a tranquil afternoon here watching farmers pick tealeaves.

Eat

Hangzhou Cuisine is known for being fresh and relatively sweet, but perhaps a bit heartier compared to dishes from Suzhou. Try **Dongpo Pork**, which is made with thick pieces of pork stewed in a rich sauce, or the interestingly named **Beggar's Chicken**, which is quite tender and delicious. For a lighter dish, try **Shrimps with Dragon Well Green Tea**, the best green tea in China.

Getting In and Out

By Air
Hangzhou Xiaoshan International Airport serves domestic flights from Beijing and Hong Kong, and international flights from Amsterdam, Delhi, Kuala Lumpur, Tokyo, Osaka, Bangkok, Seoul, and Singapore. From other foreign cities, you can fly into airports in Shanghai, as Hangzhou is just a short train ride away.

From the airport, you can take an airport shuttle for ¥20, which takes you into the city in around an hour.

By Train
High-speed G- or D- trains connect Hangzhou to Shanghai Hongqiao Station in around 50 minutes non-stop, for about ¥78. Trains with a few stops take around 60 minutes. Trains also run to Guangzhou, Beijing, Chengdu, and other major Chinese cities from Hangzhou.

By Bus
Four inter-city bus terminals in Suzhou offer regular shuttles to Shanghai, Nanjing, Suzhou, and other major destinations around China.

Getting Around in Hangzhou

Subway
There is only one line currently.

Bus
The bus is a good and affordable alternative to traveling by taxi, which is notoriously expensive. The bus announcements and information is all in Chinese, but you can use Google Maps,

which is very accurate for the city, ahead of time or on your phone to find directions and track your location.

Shanghai

This sprawling metropolis is the largest and most prosperous city in China. Over 23 million people call Shanghai home, rich and poor. The Chinese have a saying, "Shanghai is heaven for the rich, hell for the poor." And indeed, the city is alternately a fantastic wonderland filled with every pleasure imaginable, and for most inhabitants of the city, a place where they flock to from all over China, and work hard for the hopes of one day realizing their prosperous dreams.

The city is relatively young by Chinese standards. It first rose to prominence and gained an international reputation during the Colonial Era at the turn of the 20th century, when many westerners came to the specially designated "concession" districts. They lent Shanghai an international flair, leaving behind one of the richest collections of Art Deco buildings in the world. You can still see attractive buildings in classic Parisian style, Tudor style, and

1930s buildings reminiscent of the Gilded Age in New York, all of which stand not too far from the historic shikumen houses, which blend Chinese styles with European aesthetics, and are unique to Shanghai.

After some lean years under the new People's Republic of China, Shanghai has once again recovered its cosmopolitan flair since the country opened up to the world. Today, it is as modern and dazzling as Hong Kong and Tokyo, and is the undisputed financial and commercial center of China. In 2010, it hosted the World Expo, receiving the greatest number of visitors in the event's history.

Orientation to Shanghai
The city is split in two by Huangpu River – the area to the west is called Puxi, while the area to the east is called Pudong. Puxi is the older central part of the city, where the Bund and other attractions from the city's colonial past can be found, while Pudong is the rapidly developing area across the river, where most high-rises and the Special Economic Zone is located.

For this travel guide, Pudong is considered one district, while the larger and older Puxi divided into districts.

The Bund

The Bund has been the symbol of Shanghai for as long as the city was around. This famous and attractive stretch of waterfront winds along the west bank of Huangpu River for just under a mile, from Wai Bai Du Bridge to Nan Pu Bridge. Historically, this was one of the most fashionable addresses in Shanghai. Today, tourists flock here to see first and foremost the 26 buildings of various architectural styles including Gothic, Baroque, Romanesque, Classic, and the Renaissance – styles that would not exist side by side anywhere else – from the city's colonial past. There is also the "Lovers' Wall", the flood-control wall located on the side of the Huangpu River between Huang Pu Park to Xin Kai River. In the beginning of the last century, this was once the most romantic spot in Shanghai. While it may be a less intimate date place now, Lovers' Wall still provides a very good view of the Pu Dong Area with its new skyscrapers, distinct from the older style European buildings on the Bund.

Visit the Bund at sunset or after 8pm, and you'll be rewarded with a view far more beautiful than if you come during the daytime.

Beware that scammers and prostitutes tend to work this area and target tourists. Avoid contact with both to be safe.

Transit: Take Subway Line 2 to Nanjing East Road. From there, walk 7 minutes west toward the river.

Experience

Skyline Views from the Bund
There are still many fancy restaurants and bars along the Bund, offering stunning nighttime views of the skyline. Here are two favorites of locals and travelers alike:

Bar Rouge
This magnificent dance club and bar gives any venue in Las Vegas a run for its money. A terrace on the 7th floor looks over the Huangpu River and the skyline on the opposite shore. Stylish, very international patrons frequent this glowing red bar, where if you order the signature Bar Rouge drink, they set the bar alight.

There are often acrobatic and dance performances, that lend the club a very riotous and festive atmosphere. Surprisingly, Bar Rouge is posh but still quite affordable. The drinks are delicious but won't break the bank. There is a weekly Ladies' Night when ladies get free drinks.

Captain's Bar
Captain's Bar is even more affordable than Bar Rouge, with a distinctly more laidback vibe. Located on the roof of Captain's Hostel, the low-key and welcoming bar is very popular with backpackers, and younger, less pretentious locals. Grab a few pints here and settle in, enjoy the view while you get to know the person sitting next to you.

French Concession

As its name suggests, this area was once designated for French expats in Shanghai during the colonial periods, once known as the Paris of the East. Today, French Concession is one of the richest and most vibrant neighborhoods in the city. Shanghai Stadium, traditional Shi Ku Men Houses, the famous Xu Jia Hui Shopping District, and the former resident of Sun Yat-sen, can all still be found here. Whether you are looking for tourist destinations or just some shopping time, French Concession has plenty to offer.

See

Old French Concession Streets
Wealthy French and Belgians living in Shanghai would have lived on or around Huai Hai Road in the beginning of the 20th century. They left some very pretty houses that both suggest the styles popular in their native countries at the time, and the Chinese aesthetics of the day. Many of those houses are increasingly being turned into trendy designer clothing boutiques. Explore the area

between Ju Lu Road to the north and Huai Hai Road running through the center of the area, plus Mao Ming Road to the south of the Huai Hai Road. Walk along broad, pleasantly tree-lined streets and watch for fashionable youngsters hurrying by on their phones.

Transit: Take Subway Line 10 to Xin Tian Di Station.

Sun Yat-sen's Former Residence
The Father of China's Republic, Sun Yat-sen, and his wife, Soong Ching Ling, lived in this house from 1918 to 1937. The house has been converted into a museum in 1961, and tells the story of Sun's life and career.

Transit: Take Subway Line 10 to Xin Tian Di Station. The residence is located at 7 Xiang Shan Road.

Soong Ching Ling's Former Residence
The wife of Sun Yat-sen, Madame Soong Ching Ling was a respected politician in her own right, and took part in the politics of the Communist Party especially after Sun's death. As such, much state business took place here. The house has also been converted into a museum with many artifacts that focus on the politics of China leading up to the founding of the People's Republic of China in 1949. Soong was educated in the U.S. and spoke fluent English, so much of the exhibit should be interesting to Chinese and non-Chinese alike. There are also a few state-used cars in the well-maintained garage on the grounds.

Transit: Take Subway Line 10 or Line 11 to Jiao Tong University Station.

Site of the First National Congress of Communist Party of China

Located next to the fashionable pedestrian area of Xin Tian Di, the Site of the First National Congress of Communist Party of China is more austere and far more historically intriguing. On July 23, 1921, 13 founding members held the very first national congress of the Communist Part of China here, marking the birth of the ruling party today. Since opening 50 years ago, over 10 million visitors from China and abroad have attended the museum. Recent years, the number of visitors has increased dramatically after the museum was remodeled in 1999.

Transit: Take Subway Line 10 to Xin Tian Di Station.

Experience

Xin Tian Di Pedestrian Area
In the 1920's Shanghai, Xin Tian Di area was a predominantly residential area, with many traditional Shi Ku Men houses. Today, you can still admire them with their well-maintained antique walls, intricate tiles and unique exteriors, but on the inside, a different, more modern world occupies these old houses. International galleries, bars, cafes, trendy boutiques, and theme restaurants have found their homes in this historical district, turning it into a famous urban attraction for tourists, cool locals, and expats living in Shanghai. Take a walk around, shop, eat, drink, people watch, and just take in the bustling city atmosphere.

Transit: Take Subway Line 10 to Xin Tian Di Station.

Xu Ja Hui Shopping
You can find everything you need in this massive shopping district. Centered on the intersection of Hong Qiao Road, Hua Shan Road, Zhao Jia Bang Road, and North Cao Xi Road, the district is home to three supermarkets, six major shopping malls, and nine large-scale office towers. Grand Gateway Mall is the

poshest of these malls. While you can find anything from groceries to cosmetics here, Xu Jia Hui is most famous for its electronics stores. There is a huge variety of electronic equipment, from cameras to PSPs, Xboxes and other gaming consoles. Pacific Digital Plaza is the place to start. You can easily spend whole days here.

Transit: Take Subway Line 1 to Xu Jia Hui Station.

Old Town

Despite its name, Old Town is not exclusively old, but refers to the area enclosed in the ancient city walls of Shanghai, around Re Min and Zhong Hua Streets today. This district remained exclusively Chinese even during the foreign concessions period. Foreigners rarely came here in those days. Today, plenty of foreign tourists and expats come here for attractions touted as "old Shanghai", which are picturesque but rather touristy. Venture into side streets for a more authentic old Shanghai feel. Modern skyscrapers have sprang up over recent years, making up a very contradictory but unique landscape.

See

Yu Yuan (Yu Garden)
A famous classical Chinese garden on par with the gardens in Suzhou, a government official of the Ming Dynasty built Yu Yuan in 1577, as a tranquil place for his parents to retire in their old age. Indeed, "Yu" means pleasant and satisfying in Chinese.

Like its counterparts in Suzhou and other cities in this part of China, Yu Garden is laid out thoughtfully with beautiful landscaped scenery set with traditional Chinese architecture. These halls and rooms contain century-old furniture, and are decorated with calligraphy and painting masterpieces. Most think

Yu Garden is as exquisite as the Humble Administrator's Garden in Suzhou.

Transit: Take Subway Line 10 to Yu Yuan Station.

Yu Yuan Market
This market next to Yu Garden has over ten shopping streets. It's a good place to bargain for a few souvenirs or sample some well-known local snacks.

Transit: Take Subway Line 10 to Yu Yuan Station.

Temple of the Town God (Cheng Huang Miao)
Most ancient Chinese town, big or small, have a temple dedicated to their town god, used as a place of worship as well as a sort of center of market like the Forum in Ancient Rome. The one in Shanghai, located not far from Yu Garden, is quite impressive – it is the biggest and best-preserved example of traditional Chinese architecture in the city.

There is an old Shanghai saying: one who fails to reach the temple never reaches Shanghai. This is still true today. Locals still visit on holidays to pray for the protection and favor of the gods, while visitors go to the temple and the surrounding areas for both a taste of old Shanghai, and shopping and snacks in the busy streets filled with vendors.

Transit: Take Subway Line 10 to Yu Yuan Station.

Experience

Try Local Snacks and Shop for Local Goods in the Temple of the Town God Area
After 6:30pm, the area surrounding the Temple of the Town God lights up, showing off the ancient beauty of the buildings in a modern way. There are quite a few restaurants to choose from here, including some that overlook the square on Yu Yuan Road – it's a stunning view!

Jing An District

Jing An is one of the oldest districts in Shanghai. It has been inhabited continuously since the 3rd century AD. Today it is home to the old – like the famous Jing An Temple, and the new – like the famous commercial and shopping district of West Nanjing

Road, which extends from the middle of Jing An District to People's Square.

See

Jing An Temple (Jing An Si)

Jing An Temple is as famous as the Temple of the Town God and quite deservedly so. Originally built in 247 BC, rebuilt multiple times in its history, and relocated to its current site in the 1880s, this Buddhist temple is one of the top attractions in Shanghai.

There are three main halls in the temple – Hall of Heavenly Kings, Mahavira Hall, and Three Sage Hall, all filled with religious artifacts, calligraphy, painting, and sculptures from the temple's history. In particular, the massive portrait of the Sakyamuni in Mahavira Hall, measuring 3.78 meters in height, and weighing in at 11,000 kilograms, is known for the tranquil expression of the Buddha pictured – a sort of Mona Lisa of China.

Transit: Take Subway Line 2 or Line 7 to Jing An Temple Station.

People's Square

Here in People's Square is the geographical, political, and cultural heart of modern Shanghai. Bisecting Nanjing Road into East and West, People's Square was once a Colonial-era racecourse known as the "No. 1 Racecourse in the Far East." In 1949, People's Avenue was built across the area, with the square to its south, and People's Park to its north. In 1966, one million Red Guards gathered here. By the time a comprehensive reconstruction finished in 1993, this city center square covered about 140,000 square meters, the biggest public square of the city.

Transit: Take Subway Line 1, 2, 8 to People's Square.

People's Park (Ren Min Park)
Located across People's Avenue from People's Square, the park is a pleasant area that covers a total of 24.3 acres.

There are three sections in the park. In the east, there is the Memorial to the May Thirtieth Movement. In the middle area, you can find the Antarctic Stone, the Shanghai Museum of Contemporary Art, a teahouse, an outdoor theater, and a dance hall. There is also a jungle section where you can have a picnic on the stone stables, or play chess with the locals. In the west, the landscape is pleasantly curated with artificial hills, bodies of water, pergolas, corridors, and pavilions.

The park is also known for its marriage market weekly, see below.

Transit: Take Subway Line 1, 2, 8 to People's Square.

Shanghai Museum
One of the best museums of Chinese art and artifacts anywhere in the world, Shanghai Museum occupies a premiere location in People's Square. The stunning building resembles a bronze urn, highlighting the fact that the museum houses the world's greatest collection of Chinese bronzes. Over 400 pieces of the most exquisite bronze wares to have survived history, mostly from the Shang and Zhou Dynasties, evoke this important period of ancient Chinese art.

In addition to the bronzes, there are galleries dedicated to Ancient Ceramics, Paintings, Calligraphy, Ancient Sculpture, Ancient Jade, Coins, Ming and Qing Furniture, Seals, and Minority Nationalities. All exhibits are well-curated and incorporate state-of-the-art technology in presenting the artifacts artfully in world-class facilities. All information is presented in Chinese and

English. The excellent audio guide is also available in both languages.

The bronze ware of the Shang and Zhou dynasties contribute to our understanding of ancient civilization. The over 400 pieces of exquisite bronze wares cover the history of ancient Chinese bronze art.

Transit: Take Subway Line 1, 2, 8 to People's Square.

Nanjing Road
This famous 3.4-mile-long shopping street gives Fifth Avenue, Time Square, and Ginza a run for their money for all its glittering neon lights and world-class shopping. It starts at the Bund in the east, and runs west to the junction of Jing An Temple and Yan An West Street. At the center of the street is also the center point of Shanghai – People's Square.

Shanghai began to develop rapidly after the Opium War. During the concession era, Nanjing Road became alternatively the British Concession, then the International Settlement. With the importing of foreign goods, it quickly became the most fashionable shopping street in the city. In the 1930s, the street was named one of the "World's Seven Great Roads."

After decades of languishing under Communist austerity, the street has more than recovered its former glory since, attracting shoppers and people watchers from every corner of the world. There are over 600 businesses along both sides of the road, including top fashion brands like Chanel and Prada, high street boutiques, and tons of restaurants and food vendors. For those with more old-world tastes, over one hundred traditional stores still stock premium silk goods, jade, embroidery, wool, and clocks.

Sightseers can catch the trackless train for a tour of the pedestrian street, or take a leisurely albeit crowded stroll and look at the sculptures, street musicians, and some of the most fashionable people in the world. At night everything flashes neon lights, transforming the street into an even brighter spectacle.

Transit: Take Subway Line 2 to West Nanjing Road, or Subway Line 1, 2, 8 to People's Square.

Experience

Shanghai Marriage Market in People's Park

Walking by People's Park on a weekend afternoon, you may be attracted by the huge crowd of elderly people all milling about as if at a farmer's market. This is actually a weekly marriage brokering market where mostly desperate parents and grandparents of singles come looking for a mate for their unmarried child.

The Chinese have always had the tradition of choosing a suitable match for their offspring based on a number of criteria including age, height, family upbringing, income and job, mostly through friends and family relationships. This market in Shanghai acts like a dating site in real life – parents write all of the above relevant information about their child in a slip of paper, and hang it on long strings holding up similar advertisements. Afterward, they walk around looking at these papers and talking to other parents, hoping to find a good match for their child.

The "Marriage Market" takes place every Saturday and Sunday afternoon, until about 5pm, at the north end of People's Park.

Pudong District

Across the Huangpu River from the Bund, Pudong is the newest and most modern district in Shanghai. Over the last 15 years, the Special Economic Zone sprang up on farmlands and is today full of futuristic skyscrapers where financial and commercial activities concentrate. Pudong International Airport, where most foreign visitors will fly into, is also in this district.

See

Oriental Pearl TV Tower
Whether locals like it or not, this gaudy pink tower has become a symbol of modern Shanghai. It was built in 1994, and is today the 3rd tallest tower in the world. The design features 11 pink bars on its tip, the 2nd of which features an outdoor viewing platform at 259 meter. Not for the height-phobic, the platform has glass floors where you can walk onto a transparent path above Pudong and the river. A stunning view and a thrilling adventure wrapped in one! This platform costs ¥100 to experience, while the conventional observation platform in the top ball, at 350 meters high, costs a bit more.

Transit: Take Subway Line 2 to Lu Jia Zui.

Shanghai World Financial Center

The 2nd tallest skyscraper in China, Shanghai World Financial Center (SWFC) was completed in 2008 in the center of the Special Economic Zone. Three viewing platforms on floors 94, 97, 100 all offer spectacular views of the Bund, the river, and Old Shanghai. Alternatively, the 98 floor has many bars and restaurants, all offering the same view.

Transit: Take Subway Line 2 to Lu Jia Zui.

Jin Mao Tower

Jin Mao, standing just beside Oriental Pearl TV Tower, is the third tallest skyscraper in China. Inside, you'll see a 31-story atrium that rises up like a space station. There is quite a bit you can do here – an Italian restaurant Cucina is located on the 55th floor. You can enjoy a pizza while looking over the Bund and the rest of the opposite bank, for about the same price as going up the Oriental Pearl TV Tower. The 88th floor, the very top floor, also has a restaurant. The Grand Hyatt Shanghai, with Cloud 9 lounge, also offers a grand view, though at quite a price.

Transit: Take Subway Line 2 to Lu Jia Zui.

Experience

Majestic Night Views of the Bund and Old Shanghai from Cloud 9 in Jin Mao Tower

Located on the 87th floor of Jin Mao Tower, Cloud 9 is the highest you can get in a building in Shanghai, higher than the viewing platforms in both Oriental Pearl TV Tower and the SWFC. The view is amazing, but is quite pricey. Note that electricity in buildings on the opposite bank is turned off at 11pm, so the view is less amazing after then.

Transit: Take Subway Line 2 to Lu Jia Zui.

Super Brand Mall (Zheng Da Guang Chang)

This super mall has everything you'd expect – delicious food and shops of every variety. There is a flagship UNIQLO, a Toys 'R' Us, and Ding Tai Fung, which New York Times rated as one of the ten best restaurants in the world.

Transit: Take Subway Line 2 to Lu Jia Zui.

Outskirts of Shanghai

Qi Bao Ancient Town (Water Town)

There are a few ancient water towns with Venice-like canals around Shanghai, but Qi Bao is most conveniently located on the outskirts of the city, and accessible by the Shanghai subway system.

The town dates back to the Northern Song Dynasty, around 960AD. During the Ming and Qing Dynasties, it prospered into a business center with a lively economy. Today, the town is quite small, covering only around two square kilometers, but it is an open air museum of Chinese history in the region. Two canals bisect the small town, where there are many traditional houses that have partially been converted into shops and restaurants. Prices in Qi Bao are cheaper compared to the more touristy water towns, and you'll likely run into less crowd here.

Transit: Take Subway Line 9 to Qi Bao Station.

Eat

Shanghai, just like Beijing, has food from everywhere in China and the rest of the world, but its local cuisine certainly gives the imports a run for their money. Traditional Shanghai cuisine makes full use of its location on the river, which floats into the Yellow Sea, with plenty of freshwater fish, seafood, and special water plants. It is characteristically sweet and a bit oily.

"**Xiao long bao**", soup buns, are world famous. These delicate little buns contain meat and crab roe filling from Shanghai hairy crabs, with a hot, richly flavored stock that comes dripping out as soon as you bite into it. The trick is that the stock is cooled into a gelatin texture, and filled into the buns along with the meat. The heat from the steamer melts the stock again, for you drink straight out of the bun.

Another famous bun is called "**sheng jian bao**", which are a lot sturdier than xiao long bao, with a thicker skin and pan-fried until the bottom is crispy.

For a snack, try "**cong you bing**", which is a flaky pancake fried until crispy. You can find them on the street, or as a starter in most Shanghai restaurants.

Getting In and Out

By Air

Shanghai is a major travel hub for China and Greater Asia. There are two airports: Pudong International Airport, where most foreigners will fly into, and Hongqiao Airport, which serves mostly domestic flights. Be sure to check ahead of time where your flight departs.

Between the two airports, you can take a cab for about an hour, or take the cheaper shuttle buses. It is also possible to take Subway Line 2, which connects the two airports at opposite ends. The subway ride takes about two hours.

Pudong International Airport

The main international airport is located 25 miles outside the city. Arrivals are on the first floor, while departures are on the third. The airport is very sleek and modern, with all the amenities you'd expect to find in a major hub.

From Pudong Airport, take Subway Line 2 to city center, where you can connect to other lines and stations. A taxi to People's Square in city center costs about ¥160. Additionally, between 11pm and 5am, there is a 35% price hike.

Hongqiao International Airport

This airport only serves a few international flights – Tokyo Haneda, Seoul Gimpo, Hong Kong, Macau, and Taipei Songshan. Otherwise, domestic flights will likely get in here.

Subway Lines 2 and 10 take you into city center. Alternatively, you can take a cab for around ¥60, which takes you to People's Square in about half an hour.

By Train

Shanghai is a major train hub as well. There are four stations you will likely use.

Shanghai Railway Station (Shanghai Zhan)
This is Shanghai's oldest train station, serving some high-speed trains, in particular, a connection to Hong Kong. You can reach this station on Subway Lines 1, 3, and 4.

Shanghai Hongqiao Railway Station
This enormous and modern station, located in the same complex as Hongqiao Airport, serves high-speed trains to Beijing, Suzhou, Hangzhou, Nanjing, and Tianjin, among other major Chinese cities. It is on Subway Lines 2 and 10, one stop beyond Hongqiao Airport.

Shanghai South Railway Station
This station serves trains to and from the south, except high-speed trains and trains to Hong Kong. It is on Subway Lines 1 and 3.

Shanghai West Railway Station
This station is smaller, and serves some high-speed trains to the direction of Nanjing. There are also a few connector trains to Shanghai Station.

Getting Around in Shanghai

Subway
The Shanghai Subway System is one of the best in the world. Over 14 lines take you everywhere in Shanghai and the surrounding areas. The trains are very new, with English signs everywhere for the convenience of foreign visitors. You can buy a reloadable card for a ¥20 deposit. The reload machines take ¥50 and ¥100 notes.

Bus

The bus is cheaper and even more extensive than the subway. The route numbers beginning with 3 are night buses that run past 11pm, when the subway system closes. However, they are slower. Information at bus stops are in Chinese only, but announcements on the buses are available in English.

SOUTHWEST CHINA

Chengdu

Chengdu is the capital and largest city of the province of Sichuan in southwest China. It is located on the fertile plains of the Red Basin, and has had a long history of prosperity. It is sometimes known as the "Land of Milk and Honey" for its agricultural wealth.

The city contains five urban districts, four suburban districts, nine counties, and is home to 14 million people. The culture of Chengdu is considered relaxed and highly livable, unlike other major Chinese cities. It does not lack in nightlife, entertainment, and other modern amenities either.

Summer here is hot and humid. The local cuisine is deliciously spicy. The foothills of the mighty Tibetan Plateaus are just an hour to the west of Chengdu, making the city an access point to Tibet.

See

In Chengdu

Jin Sha Archaeological Site Museum
A massive archaeological site has been uncovered at Jin Sha, turning up tools and art pieces from 3,000 years ago, including pottery, blades, jade artifacts, building foundations, and various gold art pieces. The museum includes two exhibition halls: the one directly over the excavation site, and the modern display hall.

Transit: Take Subway Line 2 to Yi Pin Tian Xia Station. Get out from Exit B.

Wu Hou Temple (Wu Hou Ci)
One of the top attractions in Chengdu, Wu Hou Temple commemorates Zhuge Liang, a minister of Shu during the Three Kingdoms Period made famous by the Chinese classic novel Romance of the Three Kingdoms, and continues to be the embodiment of noble character and intelligence in China. The temple is more interesting to history buffs, since there are dozens of dust-covered statues of historical figures that the casual tourist may not find very amusing.

Transit: Take Bus No. 1, 57, 82, 334 and 335 to Wu Hou Ci Station.

Wen Shu Monastery Temple
This most impressive temple dates back to the Tang Dynasty. There is a wealth of cultural and religious relics on exhibit here, including 300 Buddha statues of various materials – iron, mud, stone, wood, and jade – from the Liang Dynasty to the Qing Dynasty. The Cang Jing Pavilion within the monastery also displays a range of historical artifacts, from famous calligraphy pieces to paintings and artworks.

After you look through the exhibit, be sure to visit the extremely famous teahouse on the temple grounds. There is no better place to appreciate Chinese tea and tea culture than these beautiful surroundings. There are demonstrations by folk artisans.

Transit: Take Subway Line 1 to Wen Shu Yuan Station.

Sights in Greater Chengdu

Giant Panda Breeding Research Base
The giant panda is arguably the most famous endangered species in the world due to its cuddly appearance. Founded in 1987, the Chengdu Research Base for Giant Panda Breeding is dedicated to protecting, breeding, and researching endangered wildlife, in particular giant pandas. From the six giant pandas the base rescued as its founding, the captive giant panda population has now increased to over 100, making it the largest facility of its kind in the world.

Aside from giant pandas, red pandas, golden monkeys and other endangered species native to southwestern China are also studied and bred here.

Visitors can see giant pandas in numbers not found anywhere else in the world here, at a much closer view than is possible at most zoos. There is also a small museum and a cinema that screens documentaries related to wildlife and giant pandas.

The base is popular year-round with tourists and school groups. Try to arrive early – by 8am when the base opens if possible – when pandas are most active just before being fed around 8:30am depending on the time of year. Around 10am or 11am, the pandas will most likely be starting a six-hour nap, so you might not see much.

Transit: Take Bus 87 or 198, or take a taxi from downtown for around ¥50 depending on traffic.

Du Jiang Yan Irrigation Project

In China, Chengdu is known as "Nature's Storehouse", providing this large country with much of the grains it needs. Over 2,200 years ago, frequent floods from the Min River, a tributary of the Yangtze River, threatened the livelihood of the residents of the area. Li Bing, a provincial official of the time, decided to construct an irrigation system to prevent flooding. After years of building, Du Jiang Yan was completed. Since then, the area has greatly benefited from the project, and has grown wealthy as a result of the irrigation. Today, Du Jiang Yan, honored as the "Treasure of Sichuan", still drains off floodwater from Min River as it has for thousands of years, and provides crucial water resources for more than 50 cities in Sichuan province.

Transit: From Chengdu Railway Station, take a half-hour bullet train to Du Jiang Yan City. From there, take Bus No. 4 to Li Dui Gong Yuan Station.

Mount Qing Cheng

Located to the southwest of Du Jiang Yan, Mt. Qing Cheng is one of the most famous and important Taoist mountains in China. The mountain itself is beautiful and lushly covered by evergreen trees. Many other peaks surround the central mountain, which is known as the "most peaceful and secluded mountain under heaven" to the Chinese.

The mountain is divided into an anterior part and a posterior part. Of the two, the approximately 15 square kilometers anterior is the more scenic. Cultural relics and historic sites dot among an alluring natural landscape. Be sure to visit Jian Fu Palace, Shang Qing Palace, and Tian Shi Cave, which are some of the most fantastic destinations in China.

Transit: From Chengdu Railway Station, take a half-hour bullet train to Du Jiang Yan City. From there, take Bus No. 101 to Mount Qing Cheng Station.

Three-Star Piles Museum (San Xing Dui Museum)

This archaeological museum, covering around one acre, displays cultural relics unearthed from the nearby Three-Star Piles site, which was an important archaeological discovery that changed people's understanding of ancient Chinese history and culture.

The site belongs to the ancient Shu culture, a precursor and ancestor to Chinese culture. The name "Three-Star Piles" refer to the three earth mounds at the site. This is a good opportunity to see some of the oldest artifacts discovered in China.

Transit: Chengdu Cheng Bei Passenger Transport Center (North Railway Station) has buses to the museum every 15 minutes.

Experience

Jin Li Ancient Pedestrian Street
This pedestrian street is considered one of the 10 best pedestrian streets in China. It is located in the old city of Chengdu. There are hotels in the ancient styles, antique shops, and souvenir stores. If you are hungry, there are also famous local snack food stalls, bars, restaurants, and nightclubs. Due to its popularity with tourists, Jin

Li can be somewhat more expensive than the rest of the city. But street food stalls tend to be quite affordable, and allows you to sample quite a few of the local delicacies before or after you visit the Wu Hou Temple close by.

Transit: Take Bus No. 1, 57, 82, 334 and 335 to Wu Hou Ci Station.

Kuan Zhai Ancient Street of Qing Dynasty
The original street of Kuan Zhai dates back to the Qing Dynasty, but much of what you see was rebuilt recently. Strolling along the street, you'll feel transported back to late Qing, and experience the local Chengdu culture. There are many restaurants, upscale teahouses, and local snack stalls.

Transit: Take Bus No. 5, 13, 43, 47 to Jin He Road, or take Bus No. 62, 70, 93 and 340 and to Chang Shun Shang Jie.

Eat

Chengdu is the capital city of Sichuan Province, which is synonymous with spicy cuisine in China. In fact, Sichuan Cuisine is one of the four most famous cuisines in China. Chengdu is the perfect place to experience some of this famous heat that has been evolving and getting hotter for thousands of years. If you are curious, ask a local about a dish you enjoy, and you are sure to learn a fascinating origin story for it.

Nearly everything here is made with the dry hot chili pepper. To cater to visitors from elsewhere in China and unsuspecting foreigners, restaurants usually offer the option of low or no spicy for most dishes. Ask for this if you are scared!

Definitely try **hot pot**, which looks like fondue, but involves meat, fish, and vegetables dipped into a spicy broth instead of chocolate or cheese. This is quick and delicious, best shared among at least three or four friends so you can try a bit of everything.

Those who have been to a Chinese restaurant in the U.S. should be familiar with **Ma Po Tofu**, but you'll want to try the dish where it's from – right here in Sichuan! Soft tofu is stewed with ground pork with plenty of chili and Sichuan peppercorn.

A famous starter is "**Fuqi Feipian**", which is cold sliced beef tripe, beef tongue, and slices of tendon, dressed in chili oil with peanuts. The ingredients might sound scary, but a good restaurant should be very skilled in making this clean and very delicious. If you are still not into offal, you can try cold diced rabbit dressed in the same flavorful sauce.

Dan Dan Mian is a well known rice dish, made with chewy fresh noodles dressed in Sichuan spices and ground pork, topped with an extra drizzle of red chili oil if you are up for it.

For the truly brave, try the various "**Shui Zhu**" dishes – pork, beef, or fish cooked in an enormous vat of hot broth. There is a thick layer of dried chilies and Sichuan peppercorns floating on top. All the meat and fish are extremely tender and flavorful, so you can't go wrong with any of the choices.

Again, this is some of the best food you'll find in China – which is a tall order for a country with great cuisine – so you'll want to try everything!

Getting In and Out

By Air
Chengdu Shuangliu International Airport is about 12 miles outside city center. It is a major hub, and serves an annual passenger volume ranked 4th in China. There are flights to and from most major Chinese cities, as well as international cities including Amsterdam, Bangkok, Frankfurt, Hong Kong, Kathmandu, London, Melbourne, Mumbai, Osaka, Phnom Penh, Kuala Lumpur, San Francisco, Seoul, Singapore, Taipei, and Tokyo.

From Chengdu Airport, you can take a cab for around ¥80 to city center. Alternatively, there are five lines of Airport Buses, running between the airport and various stops in city center, including the major railway stations.

By Train
Trains to most major cities are available in Chengdu, including Beijing, Shanghai, Kunming, Chongqing, and Xi'an. There are two train stations.

Chengdu Station (Chengdu Bei Zhan)
Even though on tickets the station is referred to as Chengdu Station, most locals refer to it as "North Railway Station", or "Bei Zhan". Most long-distance trains will arrive here.

Chengdu East Station (Chengdu Dong Zhan)
This new station serves local trains in Sichuan Province, and most high-speed trains to Chongqing. Be careful that this is not the same as the old freight station slightly east of North Station as labeled on some older maps.

Getting Around in Chengdu

Subway
There are two lines in operation. Note that you have to put your bags through an x-ray machine. Fluids will have to be checked separately.

Bus
The bus system is quite extensive. At bus stops, a screen displays the buses that will be arriving shortly. Information at bus stops and announcements on the buses are mostly only in Chinese.

Guilin

Located in the province of Guangxi, beautiful Guilin offers some of the most scenic views, and has long been one of the most popular travel destinations in China, including the Li River, with its emerald water and picturesque limestone hills, is printed on the back of the ¥20 bank note. Two rivers and four lakes surround the city, with small hills dotting through. The air is clearer here, since tourism is the city's top industry.

The province of Guangxi is an autonomous region for the Zhuang ethnic group, and is home to 11 additional ethnic minorities besides Han Chinese. As such, there is a vibrant and exotic local culture that is quite unique and different from what you might see elsewhere in China.

See

Near Guilin City Center

Elephant Trunk Hill (Xiang Bi Shan)

Majestic and tranquil, Elephant Trunk Hill stands at the junction of the Li River and the Peach Blossom River, in downtown Guilin. Its name is derived from its shape – the hill looks like a giant stone elephant dipping its trunk into the green water of the river.

This famous hill, considered the symbol of Guilin, is over 3.6 hundred million years old. It includes several scenic features like Water Moon Cave (Shui Yue Dong), which is located at riverside, and named as it looks like a full moon floating in the water with the moonlight reflected on the waves. Poets have praised the beauty of the hills and waters nearby through Chinese history. Over 70 such glowing inscriptions, mainly from Tang and Song Dynasties, can still be found on the walls in and around the cave.

There is another cave halfway up the hill from Water Moon Cave, which actually goes through the hill and looks like the eyes of the elephant from afar. There are inscriptions inside and outside this cave as well, most famously a poem by the renowned poet Lu You, one of the four greatest poets of the Southern Song Dynasty.

Transit: Take Bus No. 23 and 16 to downtown Guilin.

Reed Flute Cave (Lu Di Yan)
Nearly as well-known as Elephant Trunk Hill, the Reed Flute Cave is one of the most brilliant travel destinations in Guilin. Its name derives from the verdant reeds growing outside, which are traditionally used to make flutes. The cave was formed by water erosion, and its 240-meter length showcases a fantastic world of stalactites, stone pillars, and rock formations created by carbonate deposition, all enhanced by colored lights. It is a natural paradise.

Transit: Take Bus No. 3 or 213 to Lu Di Yan Station.

Solitary Beauty Peak and Jing Jiang Prince City
Built around the Solitary Beauty Peak on the site of a mansion of Prince Jing Jiang of the Ming Dynasty, this scenic area combines natural beauty with manmade sights.

The stunning Solitary Beauty Peak is often compared to a king, as it soars from the ground like a column propping up the blue sky. Scale the peak for the best panoramic view of the city. Among numerous stone inscriptions on the cliffs of the peak, there is a great photo opportunity at the inscription that proclaims "Guilin's Scenery Ranks First in the World." At the foot of the peak is the Peace Cave, inside which there are 60 Chinese zodiacal signs carved on the wall that are considered among the world's cultural wonders.

Transit: Take Bus No.1, 2, 18, 22, 99 or 100 to Le Qun Crossing Station.

Folded Brocade Hill (Die Cai Shan)

This park offers amazing vista and stone carvings in the northeastern part of the city. There are several peaks, which can be climbed using stone staircases. The name of the hill derives from its rock formations that pile layer upon layer, resembling folded brocade, though it is also known as Laurel Hill for the laurels that have spread across the slopes since ancient times.

Transit: Take Bus No. 2 or 203 to Die Cai Shan Station.

Seven Star Park

Named after the seven peaks in the park that resemble the stars in the Big Dipper Constellation, Seven Star Park is the largest comprehensive park in Guilin City. The park contains a variety of beautiful landscape, including elegant mountains, clear bodies of water, natural stone forests, deep valleys that do not look like they belong in a city, and plenty of animals, plants, and cultural relics in between.

The recreational area has been popular since the Sui and Tang Dynasties, in 500s and 600s AD. In particular, Flower Bridge, Putuo Mountain, Seven Stars Cave, Camel Hill, Crescent Mountain, and Guihai Stele Forest were and remain some of Guilin's top attractions.

Putuo Mountain, historically dedicated to the worship of Avalokitesvara Bodhisattva, makes up the majority of the park grounds. Its long historical and religious importance left behind a myriad of pavilions, temples, and caves. The Xuanfeng Cave at the southwestern foot of the mountain is naturally air-conditioned. Halfway up the mountain, Putuo Jingshe, a two-stories pavilion is quite pretty. The most renowned cave, Seven Stars Cave at the west belly of the mountain, with fantastic multifarious stalactites, stalagmites, and stone pillars formed by naturally dissolving limestone, is so beautiful and otherworldly that it is known as "Residence of the Immortals."

Transit: Take Bus No. 9, 11, 14, 18, 21, 25, 28, 30 or 204, and get off at Seven Stars Park.

Two Rivers and Four Lakes Scenic Spot
Referring to the landscape around the city, the Two Rivers and Four Lakes Scenic Spot is a water system in downtown Guilin bound by Li River, Taohua River, Mulong Lake, Gui Lake, Rong Lake, and Shan Lake. Like other parks in the city, this scenic spot provides a tranquil oasis away from the crowded city. For the best and most relaxing view of this area, you can take a cruise for ¥90, or ¥45 for children.

Transit: Take Bus No.2, 3, 10, 11, 99, or 100 to Yangqiao Station. Walk along Shanhu North Road to reach Riyuewan Dock. Alternatively, take bus No. 2 and get off at Lijiang Theater and then walk along Shanhu North Road to get to the park.

Yao Mountain (Yao Shan)
This large park at the outskirts of the city contains the highest peak in the area around Guilin. Its name is derived from a temple dedicated to Yao, who was one of the earliest mythical rulers in ancient China, built in the Tang Dynasty. The summit provides a stunning panoramic view of the entire area, which is quite beautiful in every season: in the spring, the mountain is covered in colorful azaleas, in the summer pines and bamboos color the mountains in emerald, in the autumn the entire mountainside is golden and red with maple leaves and chrysanthemum flowers, while in the winter snow covers over the landscape.

In addition to Yao Temple, White Deer Temple, Jade Breast Pond, and Tianci Field are also popular with visitors. Jingjiang King Tomb, which covers over 100 square meters, is one of the top attractions in the area.

A cable car takes you up to the peak. Alternatively, you can take the 1,000 meters sloping track with 18 curves, offering a different views at every turn.

Transit: Yao Shan is about 10 kilometers from city center. By taxi, it costs about ¥50.

Experience

Li River Cruise
The river cruise runs from Guilin to Yangshuo, and is a must experience for anyone visiting northeastern Guangxi Province. Being on the water offers you quite a different view of the stunning karst peaks from hiking through the mountain, as you can see the sprawling landscape against the blue sky – a special treat for China! You'll also see water buffalo grazing in the fields,

peasants working the rice paddies, and wave to children and fishermen floating by on bamboo rafts. The cruise is both a trip through nature and a glimpse into local life.

You get on board from the dock south of Liberation Bridge in downtown Guilin. The trip covers over 52 miles and takes about four to five hours. So settle in, and feast your eyes on the country scenery that is truly unique to China. If you are taking a tour, your guide will likely tell you the very descriptive names of the peaks and villages you pass. Use your imagination and see what the landscape resembles.

Logistics: You can book the cruise through your hotel in Guilin, or online at lirivercruise.net or ctrip.com. However, if you book a Chinese-speaking tour through local travel agencies, the trip will be less than half the price, for around ¥200-250.

Day Trip to Yangshuo

Very near Guilin, Yangshuo is a popular tourist destination known for the karst mountains, winding rivers, and picturesque scenery surrounding it, and the caves and temples found within those mountains. Interestingly, a large expats community has also found its way here since the 1980s, bringing some nice western-style cafes and bars with it, and a familiarity with western travelers. Most locals speak English and nearly every restaurant will have Chinese and English menus, which is very unusual for China.

Unlike most Chinese towns of this size, Yangshuo is relatively free from air and noise pollution, clean, and not congested. There are many restaurants, shops, hotels and hostels to cater to the tourists that flock to this beautiful city. You can choose to explore surrounding countryside by bike, or go hiking in the mountains. You can also hire a bamboo raft down the river for just ¥20.

Star Wars fans may recognize Yangshuo as the backdrop of Episode 3. Hundreds of limestone hills spread across the landscape that has inspired art and poetry throughout Chinese history. Among many scenic spots, Yangdi – Xingping Scenic Area, is the most popular and the traditional area to catch a bamboo raft. The rafts are perfectly safe, but be sure to haggle and shop around among the many providers when you arrive in Yangshuo. Yulong River Valley, Moon Hill, and Assembling Dragon Cave are also top spots.

Getting to Yangshuo from Guilin

By Boat
Cruises leaving from Li River take you to Yangshuo daily. Prices vary.

By Bus
Minibuses and express buses also run to Yangshuo from the square in front of the Guilin Railway Station. All buses stop at the north bus station in Yangshuo. There is no railway station in Yangshuo.

Eat

Much of Guilin's best cuisine has to do with its beautiful vista – for example fish from the Li River, or beef stir-fried with bamboo shoots from the mountains around Yangshuo. For some of the most iconic dishes, try Lipu Taro and Pork Loaf, or "**Yutou Kourou**" in Chinese, which is a traditional dish made with fatty belly meat steamed with flavorful taro and Guilin bean curd. The dish is named after Lipu County to the south of Guilin.

Yangshuo is famous for its Stuffed Li River Snails, or "**Yangshuo Niang Tian Luo**", made with river snails stuffed with minced pork, stir-fried in local spices. Li River fish is prepared in many ways, but the most popular is simply steamed to allow the freshness of the fish to really come through. If you want a heavier dish, try Yangshuo Beer Fish, "**Yangshuo Pijiu Yu**", which is Li River fish cooked whole in a local beer and vegetables.

Guilin Rice Noodles, or "**mifen**" in Chinese, is the most popular local snack. You can find these for a few bucks anywhere in the area. Locals eat it for breakfast, lunch, dinner, and every meal in-between.

The ethnic Yao people are known for their oil tea, which other locals have adopted long ago. Tealeaves are fried with garlic, salt, ginger, chili, and many other spices. The brewed result is very strong, and served with a unique breakfast cereal added to it.

Getting In and Out

By Air
Guilin Liangjiang International Airport serves flights to most major mainland cities, as well as Hong Kong, Kuala Lumpur, Osaka, Seoul, and less frequently, Bangkok. Try to book flights early for the best prices. During the off-season, tickets can be cheaper than the hard sleeper train prices, so it's worth checking both before deciding.

From Guilin Airport, you can take the airport bus to just south of city center in front of the Aviation Hotel, where you can find cabs waiting to take you elsewhere in the city. Otherwise, a cab from the airport to the city costs about ¥100.

By Train
There are two train stations in Guilin connecting to every direction in China. Guilin Station (Guilin Zhan), located in town center on Zhong Shan Nan Road, serves most trains that originate or terminate in Guilin. Guilin North Station (Guilin Bei Zhan), on the other hand, serves mostly trains passing through Guilin. High-speed trains can now take you from Guilin to Nanjing in two hours, and to Beijing in 10 hours.

Getting Around in Guilin

It is a very good idea to get a local map for about ¥5. It will show you where the top sights are, as well as bus routes that will take you to them. The bus numbers that start with 5 are free, while others are capped at ¥2 per trip. In particular, Bus #58 is useful, as it runs from the train stations to many of the attractions.

SOUTH CHINA

Hong Kong

The Hong Kong Special Administrative Region, meaning "Fragrant Harbor" in Chinese, has only been Chinese again for a few decades, as it used to be under British rule for 150 years as a result of colonization. The city developed rapidly in those 50 years, and bame the first of the "Four Asian Tigers" through manufacturing and later finance.

Today, it is a highly modernized region and increasingly a popular shopping and tourism destination for affluent mainlanders, expats, and tourists wishing to experience its fast-paced lifestyle. It is also the financial hub of East Asia, and home to many major international and local banks.

Locals speak Cantonese, a dialect of Chinese, in Hong Kong. Most people will speak at least some English, and some Mandarin Chinese.

Hong Kong Island

Almost everyone who visits Hong Kong actually only visits Hong Kong Island, where the original British settlement was located. Today, it is where Hong Kong's highest skyscrapers and its financial firms are, and the most modern and clean of all of Hong Kong territories. The poshest Hong Kong residents tend to live on the island as well. In particular, Victoria Peak is the highest point on the island, with a great view of the harbor and thus, boasts of the highest real estate prices in the world.

Central District

The center of the center of Hong Kong, Central District is home to the special administrative region's political, administrative, and financial hub. The stunning Hong Kong futuristic skyline and the wealthy Victoria Peak are both located in this district.

See

Victoria Peak

Victoria Peak, the highest point on Hong Kong Island, overlooks the entire city down below. To one side is one of the busiest harbors in the world – Victoria Harbor. To the other is the amazing skyline of Hong Kong, so magnificent that even the skyline of Manhattan pales in comparison. To the north, you can see mainland China, so close, yet for so long, remained a different entity. For your first taste of Hong Kong, get to the Peak before sundown, and marvel as the lights come on and illuminate the city. Even locals who have seen this view their whole lives never tire of it, because quite possibly, there is no other view like this in the world.

Transit: A 120-year-old funicular departs from Garden Road near MTR Central Station and takes you all the way up.

Victoria Bay and Victoria Harbor

Located between Hong Kong Island and Kowloon Peninsula, Victoria Bay is second only to San Francisco and Re de Janeiro in the world. On the bay is Victoria Harbor, bustling with the energy and restlessness of Hong Kong, the lifeline of the city. An endless stream of vessels come through the harbor amid the stunning scenery – historic Star Ferries, cruise liners, cargo ships, and wooden fishing vessels. Step aboard a Star Ferry harbor cruise for a different view of the harbor than from the Peak.

Transit: Take MTR to East Tsim Sha Tsui Station. Take Exit J, and follow the signs to the Avenue of Stars and Tsim Sha Tsui Waterfront.

Hong Kong Park

Comparable with Central Park in Manhattan, Hong Kong Park is a beautifully curated landscape amid the surrounding urban skyline, with numerous interesting sites to visit. There is an aviary with more than 80 species of birds in a mock "rainforest" environment, a greenhouse, the Flagstaff House Museum of Tea Ware, the Hong Kong Visual Arts Center, many attractive fountains, water lily ponds, playgrounds, a restaurant, and strangely, a marriage registry. These features are linked in flowing water, which runs through the park in a series of waterfalls, streams and ponds. From the park, you can take great photos of the city around.

Transit: Take MTR to Admiralty Station.

Experience

Lan Kwai Fong

Trendy Lan Kwai Fong, located between Wyndham Street and D'Aguilar Street, is known for its upscale dining and famous nightlife. Over 80 restaurants and bars crowd in this narrow L-shaped street, catering to Hong Kong's elites – famous attorneys, heads of foreign enterprises and multinational companies and top government officials. To really experience the Lan Kwai Fong atmosphere, stop by here on Friday and Saturday nights, when the best and brightest of Hong Kong all come here for long nights of entertainment. Even though many venues in the area are quite pricey, it's possible to find a good deal during Happy Hour, from 5pm to 9pm, when bars offer promotions like buy one get one free drinks and half price food. What's known as Spree Hour starts around 10pm, when university students and foreigners also join the mix.

Transit: Take MTR to Central Station.

Soho
Much like Soho in New York and London, the Hong Kong Soho area, to the south of Hollywood Road, is a fashionable district that during the day, offers many trendy boutiques, art galleries and antique shops for you to browse, and at night turn into an uproarious bars and restaurants district with some of the best places to people watch in Hong Kong.

Ride the Star Ferry from Victoria Harbor and Admire Hong Kong's Skyline
Star Ferry passes between Hong Kong Island and Kowloon Peninsula every 8 to 13 minutes. The historic ferryboats are built in an old European style, and cost close to nothing to take. From the water, the shimmering skyline is framed against the backdrop of the Peak. The nightly Symphony of Lights, the "World's Largest Permanent Light and Sound Show" according to the Guinness World Records, is amazing to behold.

East District

Tourists flock to Wan Chai and Causeway Bay neighborhoods, both located in East District along the eastern shore of the north coast of Hong Kong Island. There is also Happy Valley, where the world famous racecourse attracts visitors daily.

Experience

Jockey Club - Happy Valley

Horse racing has enjoyed a long period of popularity in Hong Kong. It was first established after the arrival of the British in 1841. The Jockey Club in Happy Valley formed shortly after, and became a professional horse racing institution in 1971. It has since become one of the top racing clubs in Asia, and is respected for its long history and proud traditions of more than 100 years.

Horse racing season here is exceedingly long – over 700 matches take place each year from early September to mid July of the next year. You can either catch a day race on Saturdays or Sundays at Sha Tin Racecourse, or a night race on Wednesdays at Happy Valley Racecourse. International first-class races are held at both venues quite frequently.

Transit: Take MTR to Causeway Bay Station. Walk for about 15 minutes to Wong Nai Chung Road.

Wan Chai District

Wan Chai District became known worldwide as Hong Kong's party district following the popularity of the 1960 film, The World of Suzie Wong. Today, it is also an attractive neighborhood for shopping and eating. There are quite a few top-notch rattan and Chinese furniture stores along Queen's Road East that will happily deliver your purchase, and some very affordable clothing stalls along Spring Garden Lane that sell garments originally intended for exporting. Wan Chai Computer Center on Hennessy is a techie heaven, while an entire street of toy stores can be found on Tai Yuen Street.

Transit: Take MTR to Wan Chai Station.

Causeway Bay
Causeway Bay is the epitome and essence of Hong Kong's consumerism culture. Everywhere you look, department stores, shopping malls, boutiques and market stalls are crammed in this compact area, catering to everything shopping impulse in existence.

For upscale clothing brands, go to Lee Gardens One & Two, Tysan Place, Lee Theater, Times Square, and Fashion Walk. SOGO Department Store and WTC Mall offer good quality mid-range choices, while the trendiest young shoppers should head to the shops on Island Beverly Center. The best bargains can be found on the chaotic Jardine's Cresecent.

Transit: Take MTR to Causeway Bay Station.

South District

For many years, the southern side of Hong Kong island were far underdeveloped compared to central and northern districts, as a result of the south-facing slopes being too sunny, and the torrential rain and typhoons that frequent here from the South China Sea. However, gone are the backward villages of the early colonial period. Today, the area has been developed into some of the most expensive real estates on the island, nearly rivaling the Peak. For visitors, ample excellent beach resorts, theme parks, and other comforts of modern life can be found here. However, the area is still distinctly different from the fast-paced bustling central district, and has more of a relaxed vacation feel, thus providing some necessary escape from city life for Hong Kong residents and tourists alike.

Aberdeen Village

The charming fishing village of Aberdeen, famous for its floating seafood restaurants and people who live on junks docked in the harbor, has been changing its image steadily over the past few decades. Originally built as a typhoon shelter for seafarers, the little village was home to fishermen and boat people for years before modernity arrived, and waterfront beach huts were replaced by high-rises. You can still find fishing boats and junks at anchor in Aberdeen Harbor, but there are just as many yachts that belong to wealthy vacationers here to enjoy the beach. Even the remaining boats are likely there to take tourists around the harbor.

Jumbo Kingdom, the world's largest floating restaurant, is located at the junction of Aberdeen Main and Aberdeen Reservoir Roads. There is a Cantonese restaurant as well as a rooftop seafood restaurant in this building.

Transit: To reach Aberdeen, take Bus No. 7 from Central Ferry Piers; Bus No. 70 from the Exchange Square Bus Terminal in the Central District; or Bus No. 72 or 77 from Causeway Bay.

Ocean Park

One of the two large theme parks in Hong Kong along with Hong Kong Disneyland, Ocean Park is a marine mammal park, aquarium, animal theme park and amusement park, featuring animal exhibits, rides and shows centering around marine life. In 2012, the park became the first Asian winner of the biannual Applause Award, the most prestigious award in the theme park industry.

The park is quite large, covering 915,000 square meters. There are two sections, the waterfront and the summit areas, connected by a funicular railway.

Transit: Take Bus 629 from Central Pier 7 or from MTR to Admiralty Station, Exit B

Experience

Hiking on Dragon's Back

Talk about a cool name! Just a short distance from the financial center of Hong Kong, Dragon's Back was voted the "Best Urban Hiking Trail in Asia" by Time Magazine's Asia Edition, and provides a great view of the surrounding areas and the South China Sea.

Transit

To the starting point: From MTR Shau Kei Wan Station Exit A3, take Bus No. 9 at Shau Kei Wan Bus Terminus to To Tei Wan, Shek O Road.

From the end point: Walk from Tai Long Wan to Shek O. Then take Bus No. 9 at Shek O Road back to Shau Kei Wan Bus Terminus. From here, public transport is available to other destinations.

Repulse Bay

This upscale residential area offers a resort-like vibe that is representative of the South District. Locals and visitors alike frequent the spacious beaches, one of the most beautiful in Hong Kong, to soak up the sun. You can also walk around and appreciate the mix of interesting architecture in this area, from the traditional Chinese style Hong Kong Life Saving Society Clubhouse with its ceiling decorated with swirling dragons, twin statues of the local deities Kwun Yam and Tin Hau, and the colonial-style Repulse Bay Building which houses designer boutiques and award-winning restaurants, as well as luxury apartments.

Transit: Take Bus No. 6, 6A, 6X, 66 or 260 from Exchange Square Bus Terminus (near MTR Hong Kong Station, Exit D).

Kowloon Peninsula

Kowloon Peninsula is the link between Hong Kong Island and Mainland China. Surrounded by Victoria Harbor on its east, south, and west sides, Kowloon is just a short Star Ferry ride away from Hong Kong Island, and is an extension of the wealthy downtown area on the main island. It has Tsim Sha Tsui, Yau Ma Tei, Mong Kok, and several other exciting areas to explore. On the ferry ride over, there are lots of opportunities for stunning pictures of both parts of Hong Kong.

See

Wong Tai Sin Temple
Unlike most other religious venues, Wong Tai Sin Temple actually pays respect to three religions – Taoism, Buddhism, and Confucianism. Perhaps because of this wide-ranging function, the temple claims to "make every wish come true upon request." Even for those without a wish, the temple's beautiful and ornate buildings set against scenic nature is quite a fantastic destination.

The temple derives from a famous Buddhist monk – Wong Tai Sin, who was born in the 4th century and was deified at Red Pine

Hill. In 1915, a Taoist priest, Liang Ren-an, carried a sacred portrait of Wong from Guangdong Province to Hong Kong. This portrait is what worshippers pray to for good fortune today.

Five of the main halls in the temple complex, each represents a geomantic element in Feng Shui: Bronze Pavilion for metal, the Archives Hall for wood, the Yuk Yik Fountain for water, the Yue Heung Shrine for fire, with the famous Buddha of the Lighting Lamp, and the Earth Wall, for earth. The brightly colored Good Wish Garden, the Confucian Hall, and the Three Saints Hall, are also worth visiting.

Transit: Take MTR to Wong Tai Sin Station, Exit B2.

Experience

Tsim Sha Tsui District
The world is distilled here in Tsim Sha Tsui's giant bazaar of stalls, shops, markets, and malls, next to the glittering harbor. Along Nathan Road, you can find anything from Bollywood-themed memorabilia to traditional Shanghainese tailors. From high-end gems and jewelry, to stalls selling high street fashion. Not to mention tons of international brands, all sorts of electronics, and any kind of restaurant you might be looking for. There are also many comfortable and posh shopping malls, like The One, K11, and iSQUARE, that offer a bit of respite from the boisterous "Golden Mile" outside. Over to Canton Road, you'll find all of the best luxury designer labels, and Harbor City, the biggest shopping mall in Hong Kong. Beyond these two roads, Tsim Sha Tsui Center and Empire Center to the east, offer tons of dining and wining options overlooking the harbor.

Transit: Take MTR to Tsim Sha Tsui Station.

Mong Kok

Another top shopping destination, Mong Kok has a different atmosphere from Tsim Sha Tsui. In these flashing streets, you can find the Ladies' Market with a network of streets, each of which has a cluster of merchants selling one type of product. For example, there are entire streets just for goldfish, flowers, birds, sneakers, and kitchenware. Outside bargain household products, you can also find electronics, cosmetics, and clothes on Sai Yeung Choi Street, Japanese and western fashion and accessories brands on Shantung Street and Dundas Street, and all-purpose malls over at Langham Place.

Transit: Take MTR to Mong Kok Station.

Hong Kong Museum of History

This museum chronicles the territory's unique past, including archaeology, ethnography, natural and local history. "The Hong Kong Story" takes visitors through the territory's past in eight galleries, starting from prehistoric Hong Kong, and ending with its return to China in 1997.

Fascinating exhibit include replicas of village dwellings, costumes and beds, and a recreation of an entire street in 1881, a tram from 1913, and film footage of World War II with recent interviews of people taken prisoner by Japanese forces.

At 11am everyday, there is a free guided tour in English.

Transit: Take MTR to Tsim Sha Tsui Station. Exit B2.

Nan Lian Garden

Designed in the style of a Tang Dynasty garden, Nan Lian is a public park and a tranquil escape from the bustling city surrounding it. All the hills, rocks, bodies of water, and plants were carefully curated. Aside from being a pleasant place to walk through, the garden offers permanent exhibits of Chinese timber architecture, rocks and potted plants, as well as a vegetarian restaurant and a teahouse.

Transit: Take MTR to Diamond Hill Station, Exit C2.

Chi Lin Nunnery
Located just next to Nan Lian Garden, Chi Lin Nunnery was established in 1934 and renovated also in the Tang Dynasty style in 1990, to match Nan Lian Garden. The large temple complex includes a number of elegant wooden halls, hosting some gold and wooden statues representing Buddhist divinities. There are also treasured relics and beautiful gardens to see.

Transit: Take MTR to Diamond Hill Station, Exit C2.

The New Territories and Outlying Islands

The New Territories cover most of Hong Kong outside Hong Kong Island and Kowloon Peninsula, including the land connecting with Kowloon and the 223 outlying islands. Urbanizing started only recently, and much of the new territories remain fairly rural. There are villages that have not changed for centuries, offering a different charm from the ultramodern sections of the territory.

Lantau Island
This island adjacent to Hong Kong International Airport is the largest outlying island in the special administrative territory, and one of the more developed. Lantau Link, connecting the airport and central Hong Kong via road and rail, opened in 1997, allowing for the development of Lantau Island around the new airport. Spend at least a day here to explore the long, sandy beach,

ample Buddhist architecture, shopping outlets, and of course, Disneyland Hong Kong.

On Lantau Island

Ngong Ping 360
Just Ngong Ping itself, which is an impressive cultural themed village, could take a whole day to explore. Start with a ride in the Crystal Cabin cable car, which features glass bottom that allows a truly breathtaking view of the blue sea and the lush green mountainside under your feet. Once you arrive in Ngong Ping, you'll find a 1.5-hectare village with interesting architecture housing a variety of shopping and dining options.

From there, take a five-minute walk, and you'll find Big Buddha and Po Lin Monastery.

At the end of the day, take the cable car back down at sunset, for another view of the stunning scenery below.

Transit: Take MTR to Tung Chung Station, Exit B.

The Big Buddha and Po Lin Monastery

The once hidden Po Lin Monastery amid the lush mountainside became famous when the Tian Tan Buddha statue – nicknamed the Big Buddha – was erected in 1993. This impressive statue is 34 meters high, and faces north to Mainland China. Though very young, the majestic Buddha attracts pilgrims from all over China and the rest of Asia.

You have to climb 268 steps to reach the base of the Big Buddha, which took 12 years to complete, but you won't regret it. The statue has a pleasing but humble countenance, with the right hand raised to bless all that come to worship. From this high vantage point, you can also enjoy a stunning view over the mountains and the sea.

Many devout monks still live in Po Lin Monastery, a very important institution that has been dubbed "the Buddhist World in the South." Take a stroll in the garden with flowers and birds, before taking lunch at the popular vegetarian restaurant.

Transit: Take MTR to Tung Chung Station, Exit B.

Disneyland Resort Hong Kong
The second Disneyland in Asia, Disneyland Hong Kong features seven magical themed lands and many of the Disney favorites. The new Disney Paint the Night Nighttime Spectacular is very special to behold: a symphony of music and color tell the stories of some of your favorite Disney characters with beautiful lights. Wave your magic paintbrush, and watch the performer's costumes change color in real time. Other special attractions include Flights of Fantasy Parade, which is a sky-high celebration with Disney characters singing and dancing along Main Street USA, and The Golden Mickeys, a musical featuring Mickey and his friends.

An advantage to Disneyland Hong Kong is that the exchange rate makes it quite cheap for most western visitors.

Transit: Take MTR to Disneyland Resort Station.

Eat

Hong Kong food belongs to Cantonese cuisine, the cuisine from the nearby Guangdong Province. As the area used to be under British rule, Hong Kong food is more heavily influenced by western cuisine than the rest of Chinese cuisine.

While in Hong Kong, you must try dim sum, which is actually a meal instead of a specific dish. People from this region gather in late morning for a big spread of delicate steamed dishes, flavorful meat dishes, and delicious east-meets-west pastries. Every restaurant offers unique dishes, but the most famous include **barbeque meat bun, dumplings with a whole shrimp**, various savory porridge, and a stinky but sweet durian dessert.

In the morning, ditch your usual Starbucks for some Hong Kong **milk tea**. This is similar to tea with milk that Brits drink, but the Hong Kong version is usually made with condensed milk, making it sweeter and more satisfying.

If you see whole ducks and long strips of pork hanging in the shop window, you are looking at "**char siu**", that is Cantonese barbeque. Barbeque pork is a classic, you can have it as its own dish, or served over a bowl of rice.

Getting In and Out

By Air

Hong Kong International Airport is a major hub. This modern and luxurious facility has been named as the "World's Best Airport" by Skytrax 8 times in the past. There are direct flights to Hong Kong from everywhere in the world. Most western cities will have at least one daily flight to Hong Kong, while flights to major Asian cities are very frequent.

Airport Express is the quickest way to get into the city. There are connections to Hong Kong Station, Tsing Yi Station, and Kowloon Station. Trains run every 10 minutes, and tickets run between $60 and $100 for single and same-day return tickets, $110 to $180 for return tickets.

S1 buses are much cheaper, and run to Tung Chung MTR Station for $3.50. From there, you can take the Tung Chung MTR Line to Kowloon, Hong Kong Island, or Tsim Sha Tsui. However, there are luggage restrictions in the MTR system.

A cab to Central will cost about $250 to $350. In general, red cabs go to Hong Kong Island and Kowloon, while green cabs go to the New Territories, and blue taxies go to Lantau Island.

By Train

Hong Kong is served by Hung Hom Station in Kowloon. There are trains to Guangzhou, Dongguan, Foshan, and Zhaoqing in Guangdong Province. The Guangzhou-Hung Hom train has two levels and is very comfortable.

You can also take the train to Beijing and Shanghai, but these are fairly long journeys.

Getting Around in Hong Kong

Consider purchasing the Octopus Card (Bat Dat Toong in Cantonese), a prepaid debit card that can be used not only for the public transit system, but also items at convenience stores, supermarkets, fast food chains like McDonalds and Café de Coral, vending machines, roadside parking, and some parking lots.

Subway
The MTR, Hong Kong's Mass Transit Railway, is the fastest way to get around, but you don't get the views like you would on trams and buses. Five lines run in the city, while three run in suburban areas. There is also an Airport Express.

Buses
The buses in Hong Kong are easy to use with the Octopus Card, but English signs are sparse. Their timetables are usually unreliable, especially in Kowloon and New Territories. You may have to wait for a long time. However, when traveling on the south side of the island and in Lantau, buses are your only option.

TIBET

Looking over the rest of China from its vantage point of over 4,000 meters, Tibet is situated on the world's largest and highest plateau – often referred to as the "Roof of the World". Aside from Tibet, the plateau borders Qinghai, Sichuan, Yunnan, and lastly Gansu provinces. Two mighty mountain ranges bound the region – the Himalayans, which contains Mt. Everest, and the Thanggulas in the north. These enclosures, and the region's high altitude, contribute to the dry and continental climate in Tibet, with strong winds, low humidity, low oxygen, and huge fluctuation in annual and summer daytime temperature. While the city of Lhasa and surrounding areas have a history as long as any place in China, some areas of Tibet are so remote and have such harsh climates that they have remained some of the last uninhabited land on earth.

In the areas that mankind has occupied, however, Tibet is a wonderland of majestic monasteries, undisturbed stunning nature, exhilarating treks and hikes, and one of the most hospitable peoples you will come across on your travels.

For those seeking a spiritual or religious pilgrimage, monasteries, prayer halls, and remote retreats dot the landscape. You'll likely find good company in devout local grannies mumbling mantras in temples, and those coming from a long distance away, having walked or prostrated themselves for thousands of miles. This level of devotion and faith is rare in today's world, and is truly a unique sight to behold.

For those looking for an adventure, Tibet's elemental beauty will not disappoint. Every view, whether of soaring glacial mountains, shimmering turquoise lakes, and boundlessly expansive plains, is sure to take your breath away. Hike through the mountains, past ruins of ancient hermitages, tents of present day nomads, and flocks of grazing animals – you are only limited by your ability to procure the permits.

Understanding Tours and Permits
Heavy travel regulations severely limit independent travel, especially for non-Chinese nationals. Foreign travellers are required to book a tour group ahead of time, who will arrange for a guide and transportation for their time in Tibet.

On the plus side, tourism is rapidly developing in the region. New airports, comfortable western style hotels, and paved road, are being built everyday and are beginning to provide a level of comfort unheard of just a few years ago.

Lhasa

The beautiful capital of Tibet is located on the northern bank of the Kyichu River, in a mountain-bound valley. First settled some 1,300 years ago by Tibetans, this ancient but remote city glitters and stuns in the bright plateau sun. The name "Lhasa" means the "Holy Land" or the "Buddha Land" in the Tibetan language, paying respect to the city's importance in Tibetan Buddhism.

Today, the city covers 30,000 square kilometers, with a population of 400,000, 87 percent of which are Tibetans. The city's unique cultural and religious heritage, its previously inaccessible location, and its splendid landscape, are now beginning to attract larger and larger numbers of tourists, pilgrims, and westerners curious about this corner of the planet. It is one of the 24 Historical and Cultural Cities of China.

See

Potala Palace

Potala Palace, situated on the Red Hill in central Lhasa at over 12,000 feet, is the highest ancient palace in the world.

The name Potala comes from a holy hill in South India. In Sanskrit, it means "Abode of the Avalokitesvara, the Buddha of Mercy." In the 7th century, the first King of Tibet, Songtsen Gampo, built this nine-story palace with a thousand rooms, in preparation of his wedding with Princess Wen Cheng of the Tang Dynasty in a peace marriage. Unfortunately, after the collapse of the Songtsen Gampo Dynasty, this magnificent palace was almost entirely destroyed in the subsequent civil wars.

The structure we see today dates from the Qing Dynasty, and has been steadily expanded since the 17th century. It is composed of two parks, the inner Red Palace at the center, and the two White Palace wings. The Red Palace, or Potrang Marpo, is dedicated to religious study and Buddhist prayer. It consists of a maze of different halls, galleries, and winding passages, including the

Great West Hall, Dharma Cave, the Saint's Chapel, and the Tomb of the Thirteenth Dalai Lama, among others. The White Palace was the residence of the Dalai Lama, and today still contains many tombs of Dalai Lama in history.

Note that visitors have to follow a strictly regulated route through the palace, and may only stay for one hour. No liquids allowed inside.

Transit: Take bus no. 1, 7, 11, 13, 20, 21, 22 or 26 to Minhangju Station and then walk to the ticket office.

Jokhang Temple

The undisputed spiritual center of Tibet and the holiest destination for Tibetan Buddhism, Jokhang Temple is a stunning live museumm of the devotion of the Tibetan Buddhist believers.

The name "Jokhang" means literally the "House of the Buddha". Situated at the heart of old Lhasa, it was also built by Songtsan Gambo for both of his wives, the Tang Princess Wen Cheng, and the Nepalese Princese Bhrikuti. The four-story building, with its opulent gilded bronze tiled roofs, is built in a combination of Han Chinese, Tibetan, Indian, and Nepalese architectural styles.

Jowo Rinpoche is the main hall in the temple, and the most revered image to Tibetan Buddhists. Hundreds of Buddhist statues and images, brought by the princesses as part of their dowries, are still kept across the temple grounds. The doorframes, columns, and finials, also survive from the 7th and 8th century.

Note that the temple is only open to religious worshipers until 11:30am. It is then open to tourists until 17:30. Groups exceeding 10 people are not allowed to enter.

Transit: Walking distance from downtown center.

Drepung Monastery (Zhe Bang Si)

Located at the foot of the Gambo Utse Mountain, Drepung Monastery is the most important monastery of Gelugpa, or the Yellow Hat Sect of the Tibetan Buddhism, and one of the "Three Great Monasteries" for the religion. It covers a massive 250,000 square meters, and was home to 7,700 monks, with 141 fazendas and 540 pastures at the height of its influence. The name means "collecting Rice" in the Tibetan language, as the white behemoth, seen from afar, looks like a heap of rice. The main buildings are Ganden Potrang, Coqen hall, the four Tantric colleges, and the dormitories.

Transit: The best way to reach Drepung Monastery is to take a taxi, as it is situated on a hill.

Sera Monastery

Along with Drepung Monastery and Ganden Monastery, Sera Monastery is considered one of the "Three Great Monasteries" in Tibetan Buddhism. It is located at the foot of the Tatipu Hill, and is dedicated to the Gelugpa or Yellow Hat Sect. Jamchen Chojey, one of the disciples of Tsong Khapa, the founder of the sect, built this monastery in 1419 during the Ming Dynasty. "Sera" means wild rose in Tibetan, since the hill behind it was covered in rose blooms.

The magnificent monastery covers over 28 acres, with Coqen Hall, College, and Dormitory. Stunning scriptures written in gold powder, fine statues, scent cloth, unparalleled murals, can be seen throughout these halls. Debates on Buddhist doctrines are still held in these halls.

Transit: The best way to reach Drepung Monastery is to take a taxi, as it is situated on a hill.

Norbulingka (Precious Stone Garden)

This pleasant garden, combining traditional Tibetan architecture and natural beauty, was once the summer palace of Dalai Lama. The name means "Park of Treasure" in Tibetan. This magnificent, with 374 rooms, cover more than 360,000 square meters. It is the largest garden in Tibet Autonomous Region.

Three main potrangs, or "palace" in Tibetan, are the main attractions – the Kelsang Potrang, Tsokyil Potrang, and Takten Migyur Potrang, built by three Dalai Lamas. These halls are decorated in many elegant statues, wall paintings, and exquisite china from China.

Transit: Take Bus 2 to Norbulingka.

Tibet Museum

The museum is located at the southeast corner of Norbulingka Palace. It was inaugurated in 1999, and is the first large modern museum in the region. A large permanent collection, containing around 1,000 artifacts, showcases magnificent examples of Tibetan art and other aspects of the cultural history of Tibet. The exhibit is divided into pre-history culture, indivisible history, culture and arts, cultural customs, politics, religion, and cultural arts.

The building itself was specially designed to combine traditional Tibetan architecture with modern aesthetics, built in grey brick with a golden orange gilded roof. The central courtyard has an attractive white floor that incorporates traditional monastic conventions.

Transit: Taxi is very affordable from downtown. You can also take Buses 86, 98, 109, 201, 203, 204 directly to the museum.

Ganden Monastery

The last of the three great monasteries in Llasa, Ganden Monastery is located on Wangbur Mountain on the southern bank of Lhasa River, at an altitude of over 12,000 feet above sea level. It is the top of the six famous temples of Gelugpa, and one of the earliest and largest Buddhist monasteries in Tibet. The annual Buddha Painting Unfolding Festival, one of the greatest Tibetan Buddhist festivals, is held here. There are over 50 structures in the temple.

Transit: Shuttle buses from the square of Jokhang Temple run directly here.

Lake Namtso
About 4.5 hours outside Lhasa, Lake Namtso, Tibetan for "Heavenly Lake", is one of the most beautiful and holiest locales in Tibet. It is so named as it occupies a high altitude, and boasts of stunningly pure blue water, and has had a long history of spiritual importance. Tibetans consider it as "next to heaven". The turquoise colored lake is set against soaring snow-capped mountains, and open grassland where yak herds and local nomads still graze. You can walk around the lake, or explore the hills

nearby. If possible, get to the lake before sunrise, or stay for sunsets, as the already stunning landscape is bathed in rose-colored sunlight at this hour. It is out of this world.

Note that the road to the lake is close between December and March. Some suffer altitude sickness at this height. Try to avoid strenuous activities.

Transit: It is easiest to drive to the lake. However, foreign tourists are required to be part of a tour group when visiting Lhasa, so choose a tour group that will take you to the lake.

Experience

Barkhor Street

Barkhor Street is an ancient round street that surrounds Jokhang Temple, and a great place for visitors to learn about the local culture, religion, and arts.

According to history, the street came about after Songtsen Gampo built Jokhang Temple in 647. The magnificent new temple attracted thousands of Tibetan Buddhist pilgrims, making a trodden path leading to the temple. This was the original Barkhor Street.

Today, you may still see pilgrims walk along the street holding the prayer wheel. Some of them are teenagers who walked thousands of miles to reach this most sacred temple. This level of piety is quite amazing to see in today's world.

For the casual visitor, there is no better place to see the old Lhasa than Barkhor Street. Hand-polished stone boards pave the street. Shops and stalls line both sides of the street one after another. You can find prayer wheels, traditional long-sleeve Tibetan costumes known as "chuba", Tibetan knives, and other religious articles here. Lovers can also find "Thangka", Tibetan scroll paintings, that are quite unique. There are also vendors selling Indian and Nepalese goods.

Eat

Your tour group will likely have many local food recommendations. But if not, ask for Lhasa **Tsampa**, which is a Tibetan staple made with pulverized highland barley flour. Locals typically serve the flour with salty **Tibetan butter tea**, stir and knead the mixture until the whole thing forms into pieces of cake.

Tibetans also specialize in **dried meat and sausages**. Nomads from the area have relied on these foods for more than 1000 years as they migrated across the plateau.

Tibetan tea is likely quite different from what you are used to, but very delicious. The most popular tea here is butter tea, which nomads have also drunk since the days of King Songtsen Gampo. Tea is brewed for as long as half a day, before it is skimmed and mixed with fresh yak butter and salt. The tea is shaken until everything mixes to the consistency of thick oil, and served in clay teapots. The taste resembles a richer and more nourishing milk tea.

With all the yak and goat you see grazing in the Tibetan landscape, it is no surprise that milk in Tibet is extremely fresh and delicious. Tibetan milk products are considered one of four treasures of the region. Also try **yogurts and cheeses** made from local milk.

Getting In and Out

Note that non-Chinese nationals traveling to Tibet are required to obtain a special permit, and must have a tour guide. For more information, refer to the Visa section of this travel guide, and the introduction to Tibet.

By Air
Lhasa Gonggar Airport serves flights from Beijing, Chengdu, Chongqing, Guangzhou, Kunming, Qamdo, Shanghai, Xi'an, Xining, and Shangri-La. There are international flights to Kachmandu in Nepal.

Non-Chinese nationals must be met at the airport by their tour guide, who will provide transportation. Chinese nationals can take a cab outside, or an official shuttle for ¥25.

By Train
The Qinghai-Tibet Railway runs between Lhasa and Golmud in Qinghai Province. From there, it is possible to travel onto Shanghai, Beijing, Chengdu, Guangzhou, Chongqing, and Xining.

By Bus
Frequent and cheap buses run between Lhasa and everywhere in Tibet, but note that non-Chinese nationals are not permitted to take them.

Getting Around in Lhasa

Foreigners are permitted to take public buses in Lhasa, which costs ¥1. However, as this rarely occurs, prepare to be gawked at during your ride. Bus destinations are in Chinese.

PLANNING YOUR TRIP

Climate

Being a very large country, China has very diverse climates. Its northernmost regions have roughly the same latitude as Montreal, with the same frigid climate, while its southern regions like the famous vacation spot, Hainan Island, have the same tropical climate as Jamaica. In general, northern China will have four distinct seasons with hot summers and cold winters, while southern China will have milder and wetter climate year round. To the west in the provinces of Gansu and Xinjiang, or in the Tibetan highlands, the climate is harsher and the land is far less inhabited compared to eastern and central China.

Best Times to Visit

Autumn
September to early October is generally the most comfortable time of the year to visit China. Temperatures are pleasant throughout China, from around 50F in the north, to around 75F in the south, with not too much rain. As a bonus, valuable ancient paintings in Beijing Palace are only displayed in September, as the climate is appropriate with low humidity and proper temperature.

Spring
Spring can be a good time to visit as well, with roughly the same temperatures as autumn. Sometimes the weather can be unpredictable, however, so be sure to bring plenty of layers and adjust with the changes.

Winter and summer are trickier, depending on where you are going. In the north and in Tibet, winters will be quite bitterly cold, while summers in the south will hot almost everywhere, and in some parts very humid and rainy.

Holidays/Festivals

There are five major holidays in China, during which time the Chinese travel very heavily. As a result, try to avoid traveling during these days so you don't have to deal with very crowded trains and flights, as well as attractions.

Chinese New Year
Also known as Spring Festival, Chinese New Year is usually in late January to mid-February, depending on the Chinese lunar calendar. This is a very busy and hectic time in China. It is the longest holiday in China, and traditionally a time for returning to one's extended family. Nearly the entire city will be shut down, so you'd be hard pressed to find anything to do or eat then. In addition, everyone will be trying to go home, making it the absolute worst time to take trains or flights, unless you are up to dealing with Chinese crowds.

Qing Ming Festival
Usually on April 4th to 6th, Qing Ming is the traditional tomb-sweeping day for the Chinese to pay respect to their ancestors. Cemeteries and other locations outside the city tend to be very crowded, and traffic out to the city will be very bad.

Chinese Labor Day
This is a weeklong holiday around May 1st, where many Chinese will be traveling. Try to avoid for sightseeing.

Dragon Boat Festival

Usually in May or June depending on the lunar calendar, this is a festival for boat races and eating "Zong Zi", steamed sticky rice in a pouch made of leaves.

Mid-Autumn Day
Taking place on the 15th day of the 8th lunar month, Mid-Autumn Day is usually in late September or early October. People gather outside to admire the full moon, while eating traditional moon cakes.

National Day and Golden Week
On Oct.1st and the following week, this holiday celebrates the founding of People's Republic of China. Nearly everyone will be traveling during this week, just like Chinese New Year, but usually to visit tourist destinations instead of their families. As such, this is a bad time to travel for tourists.

Early July and Late August
This is not a holiday, but rather when more than 20 million university students go home at the beginning of their summer vacation, and in late August, when they return to school. Trains and flights will be very jammed. It'll be hard to even get tickets.

Exchange Rates

In Mainland China, the currency is called Ren Min Bi (RMB), with the unit of "yuan", denoted by the symbol ¥.

In Hong Kong, the currency is Hong Kong Dollar.

The following rates are calculated at the time of this writing. Please check before your departure for the up-to-date exchange rate.

USD: 1 Dollar = 6.36 Yuan
Canadian Dollar: 1 Canadian Dollar = 4.79 Yuan
British Pounds: 1 Pound = 9.66 Yuan
Euro: 1 Euro = 7.13 Yuan
Australian Dollar: 1 Dollar = 4.46 Yuan

USD: 1 Dollar = 7.75 HK Dollar
Canadian Dollar: 1 Canadian Dollar = 5.87 HK Dollar
British Pounds: 1 Pound = 11.77 HK Dollar
Euro: 1 Euro = 8.70 HK Dollar
Australian Dollar: 1 Dollar = 5.44 HK Dollar

Visa Information

It is very important to note that visas to Mainland China, and those to Hong Kong and Macau, must be applied separately. Most western visitors will not need visas to visit Hong Kong or Macau, but almost everyone will need a visa to visit Mainland China. Both types can be obtained through a Chinese embassy or consulate. There is an additional permit for foreigners wishing to visit Tibet.

There are a few classes of visas to China: L Visa, for tourists, F Visa, for business trips, exchanges, and study trips, and X Visa for students. The tourist L Visa is quite easy to obtain, and you can apply for single, double, or multiple entries. Single-entry visa is usually valid for 30 days and must be used within three months of issuing. Of course, whether you are granted each type is up to the consulate's discretion.

For more information on specific requirements for the visa application, find more information here: http://www.china-embassy.org/eng/visas/hrsq. For most applicants, a number of documents are required with the application, so be sure to prepare adequately before going to an embassy.

72-Hours Free Transit
To help make international visitors' short stays in China, a number of large cities have adopted this policy to allow passengers carrying passports from 51 countries, including but are not limited to the U.S., Canada, UK, and Schengen region countries, to stay up to 72 hours without a visa on direct transit. The cities include Beijing, Shanghai, Guangzhou, Chengdu, Chongqing, Harbin, Shenyang, Dalian, Xi'an, Guilin, Kunming, Wuhan, Xiamen, Tianjin, and Hangzhou.

Tibet Travel Permit

All non-Chinese citizens must apply for a Tibet Travel Permit, issued by the Tibet Tourism Bureau. For any trains, flights, or buses headed to Tibet, this permit will be checked before you are allowed to board.

The only way to obtain this permit is by arranging for a tour operated by an approved Tibetan travel agent, and the package must include accommodations and transportation. This is important as foreigners are not allowed to take public buses across Tibet, and from the time of landing in Tibet, must travel by private transportation arranged by the tour. Generally, tour groups will have more specific information for applying for this permit, and help you with the process.

Hong Kong Visa

The immigration system to Hong Kong is separate from that of Mainland China, as well as Macau. There are border checks between these three regions. In addition, leaving the Mainland for Hong Kong counts as leaving China. So, if you visit Mainland China first, go to Hong Kong, and want to return to the Mainland, make sure you have a multiple-entry visa to the Mainland, otherwise you will not be able to return. All visitors are also required to demonstrate evidence of adequate funds, and have confirmed booking for the onward journey.

Full citizens of United Kingdom are allowed to visit Hong Kong for 180 days without a visa. Citizens of British Overseas Territories, all EU member states, United States, Canada, and Australia, can visit Hong Kong for 90 days without a visa. For more information, visit http://www.immd.gov.hk/eng/services/visas/visit-transit/visit-visa-entry-permit.html.

ESSENTIAL CHINESE CULTURE TO KNOW

Chinese culture will likely be quite a shock to western visitors. Some normal local behaviors might prove a bit jarring, but mostly these are not serious problems.

For example, people with obviously non-Chinese features will be considered exotic, and curious locals will stare, or in some cases, ask to take a photo together. Some foreigners might be greeted with a "hello" regardless of where they are from, or are referred to as "laowai", a somewhat affectionate term for "foreigners". This is rarely motivated by hostility.

In terms of sanitation, China can appear quite vulgar to westerners. Traditional Chinese medicine believes it is unhealthy to swallow phlegm, it is not uncommon to see Chinese people spitting in public. Also, it is not uncommon for small children to eliminate their bodily waste in public – in bushes, on the sidewalk, or even in train stations. Even adults do not cover their mouths when they cough or sneeze.

In general, China is not an overly polite country. In crowded situations, people are accustomed to pushing and shoving to get somewhere. For situations where people are meant to wait in line, the Chinese will usually try to jump ahead, or not form lines at all.

People will smoke everywhere, even in areas clearly labeled "no smoking allowed." However, Beijing now forbids smoking in restaurants.

Lastly, you may have heard of China's infamous censorship regime. You'll have a hard time accessing many US-based websites there, including Facebook, Twitter, and Gmail. If you absolutely need to use these sites, consider purchasing a VPN (Virtual Private Network) service for the duration of your trip.

Formalities

Saving Face
The Chinese tend to be very concerned about "saving face." So be considerate. Pointing out someone's mistake directly will cause him or her to "lose face." If necessary, try to take the person aside and tell them in private, and do it tastefully.

Pointing at Religious Statues
Pointing at statues of the Buddha and other deities with your index finger is considered very rude.

Drinking
When offered a drink in China, you are expected to take it. Otherwise, others at the table will keep pushing you. An excuse like "I don't feel like drinking" likely won't get you off the hook. Try to say, "I'm allergic to alcohol", or pretend that you are already drunk. Don't panic – foreigners are usually excused from much of these customs.

Costs

Mainland China is not as cheap as it used to be in the 1990s, but it is still quite affordable compared to western countries. If you are smart – find budget hotels or hostels, use public transit, and eat local food – you can live on a budget of around ¥200 to ¥300 a day as a traveler. However, Shanghai and Beijing are getting quite expensive, and entrance fees to tourist attractions and historical sites are increasing rapidly.

Tipping

In general, China is not a tipping country. Waiters, room service personnel, taxi drivers, and other service workers do not expect a tip, with the exception of hotels that cater to foreign clients.

Bargaining

You can still bargain over many things in China. A general rule of thumb is if a store is owned by a large company – international clothing brands, department stores, etc. – you should not try to bargain.

For almost everything else, it doesn't hurt to try! At malls with individual stalls or informal vendors, you can definitely bargain. Some restaurants, KTVs, and bars, will gladly send a free dish or two if you are spending a lot of money at the venue. In tourist shops and souvenir stalls, bargain!

For a beginner, it might be hard to know what price to offer to start negotiating. Depending on the good, anywhere from 5% to 50% is an appropriate starting point. In general, the more touristy a place is, the more discount you can ask for – 30% to 50% is common. For local places, 50% is too much. Try to walk around and compare to get a good sense of how much something is worth. If a proprietor is offering really low prices, it may be a sign the quality is not great.

Safety

Food and Water Sanitation

China has great food, so you should try everything. But be start – avoid small street food stalls unless it's in one of those famous food streets, or when you can tell it is very clean, and there is no danger of the food is undercooked. Poor hygiene can cause bacterial or parasitic infection, especially in hot weather. Try to avoid seafood and raw meat unless you are in Beijing, Shanghai, or respectable venues in other large cities. Definitely abstain from these dishes on the street in summer. As a final precaution, bring diarrhea medication, and do not drink tap water in China.

Scams
Chinese can be friendly, but avoid any locals who appear overly friendly right away and invite you somewhere. What's known as the "teahouse scam" befalls foreigners often: in a tourist destination like Tian An Men Square, or a shopping district like Wang Fu Jing in Beijing, or Nanjing Road in Shanghai, a local comes up to you and strikes up a conversation in English. They show goodwill by helping you bargain and showing you around. After, they invite you to a café, teahouse, or a pub, where every item – a cup of tea, a biscuit, or a slice of fruit – is priced at an extortionate price. You will not be allowed to leave until you pay the astronomical tab. In some cases the scammer will convince you to pay at least half of the really big bill.

A similar scam is run by "art students" who invite you to art shops and force you to buy overpriced, worthless reproductions.

Pollution
Beijing is, according to some, the most polluted city in the world. Locals, expats, and visitors are all increasingly concerned with the air quality in the city. In addition, 16 of the most polluted cities in the world are in China. Be prepared for smog, especially if you have respiratory difficulties. Note that the quality of air varies depending on the weather. For example, very windy or rainy days will usually clear the sky of smog. Locals are in the habit of wearing facemasks on especially polluted days.

Outside Beijing and other heavily industrialized cities, China's air condition is not as bad. Cities in higher altitudes, like Provinces of

Yunnan, Sichuan, Xinjiang, Inner Mongolia, Tibet, and the outlying islands like Hainan, have pretty clear air.

Getting Around

Chinese traffic is notorious, especially in Shanghai, Beijing, and Hong Kong. Luckily, these cities have extensive subway systems. Use these whenever possible. They are the easiest way to get around – much cheaper than cabs, and there is no danger of getting stuck in endless traffic.

Crossing the Street and Traffic Rules
Be very careful when crossing the streets in China, even at green lights, because traffic rules are only followed haphazardly, and cars rarely yield to pedestrians. To be safe, follow locals when a large group is crossing. If you are on your own, look in every direction!

Due to cars occupying every lane of the road, bikes and motorcycles just do what they like and drive sometimes on the sidewalk. It's not a bad idea to walk in the road at night, as it is better lit than the sidewalk.

Chinese Taxis
Depending on the city, taxis charge a ¥5 to ¥14, with around ¥2 per kilometer charge. A trip in any given city should cost around ¥10 to ¥50. There is no luggage charge, but taxis in many cities hike the price at night. You are not expected to tip.

Some drivers will try to cheat tourists, especially foreigners, by taking a longer route, but this is not as common any more and should not be a problem. Usually, the price difference is minimal. But if you do feel seriously scammed, you can try to apply to the doorman at your hotel. It will likely only take a few sharp words for the driver to owe up to the deception.

Public Bathrooms
Outside major cities, going to a public bathroom can be unpleasant, or even repulsive. Carry your own packet of tissue paper since toilet paper is rarely provided, even if you had to pay to use the public bathroom – usually no more than one or two yuan.

More often than not, Chinese public bathrooms are equipped only with the squatting type of toilet, which may be a bit tricky for foreigners to use.

SURVIVAL CHINESE PHRASES

Mandarin Chinese is the official language of China. However, there are over 2,000 dialects in use in China, and in cities outside Beijing, you may hear the local dialect more than Mandarin.

Older Chinese most likely do not speak English, but more and more of the younger generation has been learning English in school for years. In smaller cities, fewer people will be able to speak Chinese.

To help getting around in China, try to learn a few basic phrases, and consider downloading a translator app like Google Translate, for when you are really in a bind trying to communicate with a loca.

In Hong Kong, the official language is Cantonese Chinese, but most people speak some Mandarin, and more people compared to the Mainland will speak a good amount of English.

Yes	shì
No	bú shì
Thank you	xiè xiè
Thank you very much	fei- cháng gàn xìe / hen gàn xìe
You're welcome	bu yong xie
Please	qing (ching)
Excuse me	qing (ching) ràng, dui bu qi
Hello	Ni hao
Goodbye	zài jiàn
So long	zài jiàn

Good morning	zao an-.
Good afternoon	wu an-.
Good evening	wan shàng hao.
Good night	wan an-.
I do not understand	wo bù míng bái / wo bù dong
How do you say this in [English]?	zhe yòng [yi-ng yu] zen me jiang?
Do you speak ...	ni hùi jiang ... ma?
English	yi-ng yu.
French	fá yu.
German	dé yu.
Spanish	xi- bán yá yu.
Chinese	pu to-ng hùa / hàn yu.
I	wo.
We	wo mén
You (singular, familiar)	ni.
You (singular, formal)	nín
You (plural)	ni mén
They	ta- mén
What is your name?	ni jiào shen me míng zi?
Nice to meet you.	hen gao- xìng yù jiàn ni.
How are you?	ni hao ma?
Good	hao.
Bad	bù hao.
So so	hái hao.
Wife	qi- zi.
Husband	zhàng fu-.
Daughter	nü er
Son	ér zi
Mother	ma- ma

Father	ba- ba
Friend	péng you.
Where is the bathroom? Where is the toilet?	xi shou jian- zai- na li?
zero	líng
one	yi-.
two	èr
three	san-.
four	sì
five	wu.
six	lìu
seven	qi-.
eight	ba-.
nine	jiu.
ten	shí
eleven	shí yi-.
twelve	shí èr
thirteen	shí san-.
fourteen	shí sì
fifteen	shí wu.
sixteen	shí lìu
seventeen	shí qi-.
eighteen	shí ba.
nineteen	shí jiu.
twenty	èr shí
twenty one	èr shí yi-.
thirty	san- shí
forty	sì shí
fifty	wu shí
sixty	lìu shí

seventy	qi- shí
eighty	ba- shí
ninety	jiu shí
one hundred	yì bai.
one thousand	yì qian.
one million	yì bai wàn
How much does this cost?	zhe duo- shao qián?
What is this?	zhe shi shen me?
I'll buy it.	wo mai.
I would like to buy ...	wo yào mai ...
Do you have ...	ni you méi you ...
Do you accept credit cards?	ni jie- shòu xìn yòng ka ma?
Open	kai-.
Closed	guan-.
Postcard	míng xìn piàn
Stamps	yóu piào
A little	yi dian(r) er
A lot	hen duo-.
All	quán bù
Breakfast	zao can-.
Lunch	wu can-.
Dinner	wan can-.
Vegetarian	sù shí zhe.
Kosher	yóu tài hé fa shí wù
Cheers!	gan bei
Please bring the bill.	qing jíe zhàng.
Bread	miàn bao-.
Beverage	yin liào
Coffee	ka- fei-.
Tea	chá

Juice	guo zhi-.
Water	shui.
Beer	pí jiu.
Wine	jiu.
Salt	yán
Pepper	hú jiao-.
Meat	roù
Beef	niú roù
Pork	zhu- roù
Fish	yú
Poultry	jia- qin.
Vegetable	cài
Fruit	shui guo.
Potato	ma líng shu.
Salad	sa- là
Dessert	tián pin.
Ice cream	bing- qi- lín / xue gào
Where is ...?	... zai na li?
How much is the fare?	che- fèi duo shao?
Ticket	piao
One ticket to ..., please.	yì zha-ng qù ... de piào.
Where are you going?	ni qù na li?
Where do you live?	ni zhù zài na li?
Train	huo che-.
Bus	gong- gòng qì che- / gong- che-.
Subway, Underground	dì tie.
Airport	fei- ji- chang.
Train station	huo che- zhàn
Bus station	gong- gòng qì che- zhàn / gong- che- zhàn

Subway station, Underground station	dì tie zhàn
Departure	chu- jìng
Arrival	rù jìng
Car rental agency	chu- zu- qì che chang.
Parking	tíng che- chang.
Hotel	lü' guan.
Room	kè fáng
Reservation	yù dìng
Are there any vacancies for tonight?	jin- wan you méi you kong-fáng?
No vacancies	kè man / méi you kong- fáng
Passport	hù zhào
Left	zuo.
Right	yòu
Straight	zhí
Up	shàng
Down	xià
Far	yuan.
Near	jìn
Long	cháng
Short	duan.
Map	dì tù
Tourist Information	liu yóu wèn xún chù
Post office	yóu jú
Museum	bó wú guan.
Bank	yín háng
Police station	jing chá jú
Hospital	yi- yuàn
Pharmacy, Chemists	yào fáng
Store, Shop	diàn

Restaurant	jiu lóu
School	xúe xiáo
Church	jiào táng
Restrooms	xi shou jian-.
Street	jie-.
Square	fang-, guang chang
Mountain	shan-.
Hill	shan- / qiu-.
Valley	shan- gu.
Ocean	hai, yang
Lake	hú
River	hé
Swimming Pool	yóu yong chí
Tower	ta.
Bridge	qiáo
What time is it?	jí dian zhòng le?
7:13, Seven thirteen	qi- dian shí san- fen-.
3:15, Three fifteen	san- dian shí wu fen-.
3:15, A quarter past three	san- dian yí kè
11:30, Eleven thirty	shí yi- dian san- shí fen-.
11:30, Half past eleven	shí yi- dian bàn
1:45, One forty-five	yi- dian sì shí wu fen-.
1:45, A quarter till two	yi- dian sì shí wu fen-.
Day	rì / tian-.
Week	xing- qi-.
Month	yùe.
Year	nián.
Monday	xing- qi- yi-.
Tuesday	xing- qi- èr
Wednesday	xing- qi- san-.

Thursday	xing- qi- sì
Friday	xing- qi- wu.
Saturday	xing- qi- liù
Sunday	xing- qi- rì / xing- qi- tiàn
January	yi- yùe
February	èr yùe
March	san- yùe
April	sì yùe
May	wu yùe
June	liù yùe
July	qì yùe
August	bà yùe
September	jiu yùe
October	shí yùe
November	shí yi- yùe
December	shí èr yùe
Spring	chun-.
Summer	xià.
Fall, Autumn	qiu-.
Winter	dòng.
Today	jin- tian-.
Yesterday	zúo tian-.
Tomorrow	míng tian-.
Birthday	sheng- rì
Happy Birthday!	sheng- rì kuài lè!

CONCLUSION

We hope this pocket guide helps you navigate China and find the most memorable and authentic things to do, see, and eat.

Thank you for purchasing our pocket guide. After you've read this guide, we'd really appreciate your honest book review!

Sincerely,
The Wanderlust Pocket Guides Team

CREDITS

Cover design by Wanderlust Pocket Guide Design Team

Wanderlust Pocket Guides

COPYRIGHT AND DISCLAIMER

Made in the USA
Middletown, DE
23 June 2016